GOOD

GUILT

Kelly McCuaig

GOOD

GUILT

Reclaim the Treasure of *Hope*
at the Heart of a *Repentant* Life

 invite
PRESS
Plano, Texas

TABLE OF CONTENTS

Part V Make Repentance Cool Again (Chapters 17–20)

Part VI Embracing Good Guilt

HOW TO USE THIS BOOK

This book is meant to be flexible. You can read it at your own pace, pausing when needed to reflect, pray, or journal. If you prefer a more structured approach, try going through one *Part* each week. Each *Part* has four short chapters, and at the end of each *Part*, you'll find a *Check-In*—a space for reflection, prayer, and honest assessment of your spiritual growth.

For those participating in a small group setting, you'll find *Discussion Guides* in the back of the book that correspond with each *Part*. These guides are perfect for weekly group meetings (one *Part* each week), encouraging honest conversations and collective spiritual renewal. Additionally, every chapter ends with a *Journal Prompt*—a chance to go beyond ideas and apply them to real life. These prompts are especially meaningful when used alongside your personal devotion time or shared during small group discussions.

However you choose to read—whether alone, with a group, quickly or slowly—my prayer remains the same: that you would draw closer to the heart of God through a lifestyle of repentance. This book is not about guilt for guilt's sake; it's about discovering the goodness of guilt that leads to renewal. My deepest desire is that as you respond to the Spirit's gracious conviction, your own life of faith would be revived—and through you, your church might be prepared for an outpouring of the Holy Spirit.

Part I

REDISCOVERING
REPENTANCE

CHAPTER 1 | REVIVING REPENTANCE

What if guilt is actually good?

Walk into any bookstore, and one of the largest sections will likely be *self-help*, filled with books promising a better life. I wonder how many of those books would start with what we're starting with—guilt, confession, and repentance.

What if we once again need the conviction of sin that first led us to Christ? Instead of another consultant or program, perhaps we should return to God's plan. Even those who are already following Jesus might need to revisit the steps of repentance we first took to discover God's best for us today.

How Revival Begins

Many of you have already heard of, read about, or even attended the Asbury Outpouring in February of 2023. For sixteen days, tens of thousands descended upon the small town of Wilmore, KY to witness firsthand the hope, promise, and healing God was doing in Hughes Auditorium on Asbury University's campus. Stories abound about the renewed life in Christ that multitudes experienced during those two weeks. But less has been said about what happened the evening before. Revival in Wilmore wasn't birthed out of thin air. An honest experience of repentance was there at the beginning.

The night before, some members of Asbury's Gospel Choir gathered for an event honoring Black History Month. This gathering featured the solemn reading of names of enslaved individuals recorded in pre-Civil War estate documents from central Kentucky. As each name was spoken, the weight of history became deeply personal. Although these men, women, and children lived more than a century ago, their names served as a reminder of their God-given dignity, long denied by those who enslaved them. A sense of sorrow filled the room, not only as the students remembered that suffering but also as they acknowledged the brokenness of a world in need of redemption. One eyewitness of this gathering, Sarah Thomas Baldwin (Vice President of Student Life at Asbury University), later reflected on the atmosphere of the room: "The presence of Jesus [abided] in *the grief, lament, and confession,* taking up residence in the remembrance of suffering. People dispersed, but the holy moment… [lingered] with all of us."[1]

Some of those who dispersed, that holy moment of repentance lingering with them, went to their next event, Gospel Choir rehearsal. And what were they rehearsing for? To help lead worship for the Asbury University Chapel service the next day: Tuesday, February 8, 2023, the very chapel service at which the now famous Outpouring broke out. At that service, after the faithful Gospel message preached by Pastor Zack Meerkreebs on Romans 12:9–21 concluded, and after the student body was dismissed to return to class, three members from the Gospel Choir "lingered to continue singing" with "several dozen students praying at or near the altar."[2] Thus began the Asbury Outpouring.

So, I wonder… what if revival begins not with curriculum, programs, or performances but with hearts primed and ready with repentance lingering within our souls, as in Wilmore in February 2023?

Society's Resistance to Guilt

Let's be honest: none of us likes admitting when we're wrong or acknowledging our mistakes. It feels unpleasant, so we avoid it. Our culture increasingly values evasion over accountability. This trend is evident among celebrities, influencers, politicians, and ourselves.

It's not just our greater society that struggles to admit wrongdoing; this extends to us, the American church. Pastor and commentator Tim Challies observes that the church in the U.S. is drifting headlong into a resistance to genuine, heartfelt confession. He notes, "Our society so hates the idea of repentance, [that] many churches, out of a so-called 'seeker sensitivity,' have stopped speaking about it…."[3]

As followers of Christ, have we succumbed so much to a secular culture that we've abandoned the vital practice of repentance in our spiritual journey? If so, what benefits have we gained from this drift away from sincere acknowledgment of guilt? Are our churches fuller? Is our society more rooted in Christian values? Are more people coming to know Jesus? Are we feeling more hopeful about the future of our congregations?

---

1. Sarah Thomas Baldwin, *Generation Awakened* (Plano, TX: Invite Press, 2024), 168. Emphasis added.

2. Mark R. Elliot, *Taken By Surprise: The Asbury Revival of 2023* (Franklin, TN: Seedbed, 2023), 10.

3. Tim Challies, "Repentance and Evangelicalism," *Challies* (blog), October 3, 2005, https://www.challies.com/articles/repentance-and-evangelicalism/.

I wonder if, in a world that avoids guilt, God invites us to embrace it as a pathway to joy?

Repentance as the Path to New Life

Throughout this book, we're going to be spending quite a bit of time in 1 John, but for now, let me remind us of this verse, which shatters all of our cultural perceptions about honestly admitting guilt: "If we confess our sins, he who is faithful and just will forgive us our sins and cleanse us from all unrighteousness" (1 John 1:9). This is scripture directed *to Christians*! This is not a passage for unbelievers. This passage is written for those who have already come to faith in Jesus Christ, like you and me.

Repentance isn't just how we become Christians; it's how we stay Christians.

Repentance isn't just how we become Christians; it's how we stay Christians. And, as we follow this biblical teaching, we reap what is promised, not shame and despair for what we've done wrong. No, what we experience through an honest expression of guilt through repentance is the joy, hope, and newness of life that comes from being cleansed of sin and propelled further into the righteousness of Christ himself! Did those at the Asbury Outpouring leave with despair or new life? Repentance in Wilmore didn't lead to gloom and doom. Repentance in Wilmore led to new hope and opportunity in Jesus!

Good Guilt as God's Gift

This notion of guilt as something good to experience is not a theological concept from a New Testament letter, nor is it simply an anecdotal illustration from Wilmore, KY. Scripture is filled with extraordinary, true stories of God doing new things in the lives of his people through repentance.

Consider King Josiah, who ruled Jerusalem 2,500 years ago. For generations, the people of Israel had failed to follow the ways of God. Idols were being worshiped, the sacred space of the temple had been defiled, and no one, and I mean *no one,* was reading God's holy scriptures. It had been so long since anyone had read the scriptures that no one even remembered they existed. Until one day, some workers were cleaning up in the temple storage unit, and low and behold, there it was—the "book of the law in the house of the LORD!" (2 Kings 22:8)

3

King Josiah was quickly informed of this discovery, the scroll was brought to him, he read it, and we're told in 2 Kings 22:11 that he "tore his clothes," an ancient sign of lament before God. Josiah's repentance led the entire nation to follow. Idols were crushed, the temple was cleansed, and people's hearts were once again turned *away* from sin and *toward* their God. This isn't the sort of toxic shame that paralyzes us at the very thought of it (more on the difference between guilt and shame in a later chapter); this biblically based reality of good guilt is an experience that leads to abundant joy. Repentance didn't burden Josiah and his kingdom; repentance liberated and transformed them! Guilt was good for them.

Repentance and Revival

Many leaders will say that repentance precedes revival. What has been made less clear, in my experience, is that the repentance that precedes revival is not repentance from the masses of unbelievers. The repentance that precedes revival has consistently been the corporate repentance of believing Christians.

Consider Pastor Duncan Campbell and his church on the Isle of Lewis off the coast of Scotland. From 1949 to 1952, this entire island system of the Hebrides experienced revival. And how did the revival begin? It wasn't because Pastor Campbell yelled "Repent!" on a Scottish street corner. Instead, Pastor Campbell and a tiny group of Christians gathered in prayerful confession and expectantly waited for God's movement. The result? Pastor Campbell reported "wave after wave of divine consciousness" coming over him and "the love of the Savior" overwhelming his whole being. Again, repentance didn't bring doom and gloom to Duncan Campbell and his small repentant congregation; it brought hope and promise, and for three years, the entire area experienced a revival that brought new hope to believing Christians and new life to many more unbelievers, who surrendered their lives to Christ in the hundreds. Repentance in Pastor Campbell's small prayer gatherings changed their hearts and prepared the soil of the entire land for revival to take root.[4]

Revival Awaits

I wholeheartedly believe repentance is foundational to joy, renewal, and a deeper connection with God for our lives and churches. The story of Asbury's Outpouring reminds us that revival often begins in the quiet, unassuming

---

4. Mark Nysewander, *Revival Rising* (Franklin, TN: Seedbed, 2016). Many of the historical examples of revival I'll share in this book can be found in this excellent text by Pastor Nysewander.

moments of honest repentance. Guilt over where we've strayed from God is not a burden to flee from but a divine invitation—a gift that draws us back to His grace.

If we genuinely desire renewal and revival in our time, we must ask: Are we ready to embrace the transformative power of good guilt? Will we take the humble steps of repentance and rediscover the joy that comes when we lean into God's renewing grace?

Journal Prompt

As you proceed through this book, you will find chances to pause, reflect, and engage with themes of repentance and renewal. Journaling allows you to process through these ideas, helping you move beyond reading to experience the transformative power of repentance. Through honest self-reflection, identify areas where God calls you to grow, and embrace the hope and joy He offers. Take your time with these prompts; they are invitations to experience God's grace in meaningful ways.

- **Your Understanding of Repentance:** How do you view repentance: as a one-time event or an ongoing journey? How might your relationships with God and others change if you see repentance as a continual pathway to joy and renewal?

CHAPTER 2 | THIS ISN'T A CRAZY IDEA; I PROMISE!

When my mom graduated from High School, she received a beautiful new watch as a gift. She cherished this watch. Years later, the watch vanished without a trace. Like many lost treasures, she forgot about it.

Over a decade later, our family visited my grandparents at their cabin in the mountains of southern New Mexico. While out on their gravel driveway, my grandfather saw something shiny. He bent down to pull this shimmering object out of the gravel and out came my mom's college graduation watch! Overjoyed but doubtful, she assumed the watch was ruined by years in the elements. However, they took it inside, cleaned it, wound it up (no battery needed), *and it started to tick!* This treasure, long forgotten, now found, wasn't useless. It worked precisely as it always had.

Repentance is something that we often forget. Once we've repented of sin and turned to Jesus that initial time, we get out of the practice of confessing our sins because "we're in." We don't practice repentance in our day-to-day lives with Jesus. But repentance, like my mom's watch, while lost and forgotten in many lives, still works when rediscovered—offering us freedom and renewal.

Grounded in Scripture

One of the very first words we hear from Jesus in the Bible is "Repent…" (Matthew 4:17). But, as I've already cautioned, this is not just a call to those who have not yet decided to follow Jesus as Lord. The Gospel guides us to repentance and new birth—but that's only half the story. In that moment of repentance, God indeed secures our place in heaven, but the other half of the Gospel is God longing to get heaven *into* us today, right here and now!

Repentance secures not just eternity with Christ but also his grace in our daily lives. One day, he turned to his disciples who were already walking with him 2,000 years ago and called them to change their ways and become more like children (Matthew 18:3). This idea of changing from one way of life to another is deeply rooted in the biblical notion of repentance.

Paul continually urged believers to turn from old ways and follow Jesus. Remember, Paul's letters weren't written to non-Christians or addressed to the pagans of the day. Anytime Paul calls people to live differently, these are callings for day-to-day Christians like you and me.

Paul even touches on the paradoxical relationship between the negative connotations behind guilt and the favor of God to work through it. In one letter, he writes that "godly grief produces a repentance that leads to salvation and brings no regret..." (2 Corinthians 7:10). In other translations, the word Paul used here for "grief" is often interpreted as sorrow. It's almost as if Paul himself would look at the guilt that comes from honest reflection and conviction by the Holy Spirit as something good, very good, to experience. And when it comes from the Lord, this grief, sorrow, and guilt doesn't lead to regret but to salvation! Good guilt is nothing new; we're not reinventing the wheel here. Good guilt and the new life that comes from it are all over our holy scriptures. Like digging a treasured watch out of the ground, maybe it's time we dig repentance out from being lost and forgotten and see how powerfully it still works.

Grounded in Church History

The call for continual repentance is both biblical and historical. My own tradition of Methodism, which is perhaps the tradition of some reading this book, would have never gotten off the ground had its founders and early participants not heard God's call to continual repentance. We may not know how often John Wesley prayed in repentance, but his life reflected it. During many seasons of Wesley's life, he was known to have received Holy Communion four to five times per week, and as any good Anglican, part of this communion service would have *always* included a prayer of confession. Consider the repentant words Wesley repeatedly prayed during Holy Communion: "We are not worthy so much as to gather up the crumbs under thy table... Grant us therefore, gracious Lord, so to eat the flesh of thy dear Son Jesus Christ and to drink his blood, that our sinful bodies may be made clean...."[1]

Though revival involves multitudes, it often begins with the repentance and confessional hearts of just a few. As I've hinted here, and as we'll see soon enough, the Methodist Revival was no different. John Wesley himself, like countless others, saw renewal in his own life born out of a life of humble repentance. Throughout Methodist history and the history of the church, re-

---

1. *Book of Common Prayer* (Cambridge, 1770), http://archive.org/details/bookofcommonpray00chur.

pentance has proven to be the ignition point for transformation—personally, spiritually, and communally.

Still Relevant Today

Leaders within Methodism have noted that repentance has nearly vanished from their denomination, one leader stating, "[it] has almost completely disappeared from the preaching of [Methodist churches]."[2] We need this message today because we're failing at it! Why? Because our culture resists it. Fallen, human nature values comfort over repentance. We don't like the prosect of having to humble ourselves, honestly self-reflect, and genuinely admit when we've done something wrong. It just doesn't feel good, so we don't do it.

Yet God designed us to walk through good guilt. God, in all His majestic creative powers, designed our souls and psyches to heal, grow, and experience true joy and happiness if we were humble enough to trust Jesus' call to repent. When we rediscover repentance, we uncover a God-given treasure that still works, heals, and transforms.

Tried and True

Repentance is not outdated; it is a profoundly biblical and relevant practice today. It is the call of Christ from the beginning of his ministry, echoed in the writings of Paul, lived out in the early church, and proven through countless revival movements in history. Again and again, repentance sparks personal and communal renewal. So, what if we actually embraced repentance as the path to that renewal in our lives and churches?

Journal Prompt

- **A Forgotten Gift:** Like the lost watch rediscovered and restored, is there a specific habit, attitude, or relationship in your life where God may be calling you to the "forgotten treasure" of repentance? How might returning to this practice bring freedom, healing, or renewed joy in your walk with Him?

---

2. Walter Klaiber and Manfred Marquardt, *Living Grace: An Outline of United Methodist Theology* (Nashville, TN: Abingdon Press, 2002), 239.

CHAPTER 3 | CREATED TO REPENT

God's creation amazes me—from the stars above to the depths below, including us. God is not only wonderful in His creation; He is merciful too. Consider our bodies' ability to physically heal. When we cut ourselves, something remarkable happens beneath the surface. Blood cells rush to the site, forming a clot to stop the bleeding, and a scab begins to develop, protecting the wound like a natural bandage. Underneath, new cells multiply and rebuild the damaged tissue. Over time, the scab falls away, revealing fresh, healed skin. Originally, our bodies didn't need this healing. God breathed life into us in a day and age when there was no crying, no pain, no death, no cuts that needed scabs, no scars to reveal past wounds. Yet, in His mercy, God still created our bodies with this ability.

I believe there's another way that God mercifully created our bodies to heal. This healing isn't the healing of physical wounds but of spiritual wounds. Just as our bodies are made to recover from physical wounds, our souls are made to heal when we turn to Him in repentance. Though repentance wasn't needed in Eden, God mercifully provided the possibility of it for our healing. From creation onward, humanity has been wired to turn back, realign, and renew—it's God's built-in pathway to flourishing within each of us.

Unhindered Devotion to the Lord

It sounds so nice, doesn't it? *Unhindered devotion to the Lord*—Paul longed for the Corinthian church to have this (1 Corinthians 7:35). As he looked at a church in crisis, and as he longed for their utmost flourishing and abundant life, this was part of his prescription. Paul saw this devotion as God's original intent and rescue plan through Christ. And now, in Christ, we believe such devotion is possible!

Seventeen hundred years later, when reflecting on these very words in a sermon on the same passage, John Wesley wondered what leads a person to such unhindered devotion to God. He suggested, "They should begin with repentance, the knowledge of themselves; of their sinfulness, guilt, and helplessness."[1] In that same sermon, he said that ignoring this call to repentance is most often the "one mistake" that so many Christians make in their daily pursuit of God.

Jesus restored the devotion lost in Genesis 3. In coming to Jesus through that initial place of repentance, the promise of such unhindered devotion is placed in our hands. However, for many of us, that's where it stays as an unrealized promise. Are we ok with settling for just an unrealized promise? God isn't! He longs for us to see this promise of unhindered devotion unwrapped and made real and present for each of us. Such a realization begins, as Wesley noted, with truly knowing ourselves, warts and all.

A Positive Approach

I still sometimes feel anxiety about exposing my soul to God; *do I really want to face the mess inside me?* But what if this hesitancy of mine, and likely of yours too, is because I can't fully comprehend how incredible it would be to experience the inner healing that is really and truly possible from a life of continual repentance? A new field of research is showing just how beneficial good guilt is in our lives.

I affirm the view of my denomination that the holy scriptures of the Old and New Testaments contain all things necessary for salvation in Christ our Lord. I don't need new research to exist for God's promise of new life born of repentance to be true. Yet God graciously affirms this truth all around us, and one area where we see this confirmation is in Psychology. This field reveals how self-examination and repentance aren't burdens—they're essential tools for a flourishing life of healing, growth, and renewal.

Positive Psychology (a new subset of psychology and hereafter referred to as PP) is relatively new. Early psychology focused on mental illness, human potential, and fulfillment. However, after World War II, with an abundance of soldiers coming back home with unprecedented psychological trauma, the world of psychology shifted from that holistic approach to a "disease" mindset almost overnight, focusing solely on curing mental illness. This shift was necessary then, but psychology still focuses on repair at the expense of flourishing.

The idea of a long, painful healing process doesn't appeal to me. But what if God wants not just to heal me but also to transform me? Psychologist and fellow follower of Jesus, Charles Hackney, describes the goal of PP in a way

---

1. John Wesley, "On Dissipation," Wesley Center Online, accessed October 15, 2021, https://wesley. nnu.edu/john-wesley/the-sermons-of-john-wesley-1872- edition/sermon-79-on-dissipation/.

that I believe could powerfully describe our own goal as Christians in following Jesus:

> Think of a scale ranging from negative ten to positive ten, with negative ten being the lowest possible depths of misery, the zero point being neutral (neither doing poorly nor doing well), and positive ten being the happiest life possible. Currently, psychology is good at helping people who are around negative six or negative seven to make it up to the neighborhood of zero (maybe positive one on a good day). By contrast, we know very little about how to help people get from the zero point to positive seven.[2]

In my experience, the American church often settles for getting people to zero. They're no longer trapped in the depths and misery of their own sin. They profess faith in Jesus Christ. They're "safe." And, like the field of psychology, they are all too satisfied to stick with that result because the disease has been cured. The goal has been met.

But what if God wants more? How do we move from zero to ten in faith? I wonder if the challenges PP sets out for its field should also be the ones we set for ourselves. What is God showing us about His amazing creation of the human brain through the exciting research happening in PP, and how does this align with what we know to be true from scripture, that "If we confess our sins, he who is faithful and just will forgive us our sins and cleanse us from all unrighteousness" (1 John 1:9)?

I think the connections between what we're learning in PP and what God promises in scripture are astounding. One study found that "people who experience greater guilt in response to specific transgressions or conflict episodes also report better long-term outcomes."[3] Another study examined the effect of partial confession versus full confession: "…people seeking redemption by partially admitting their big lies feel guilty because they do not take complete responsibility for their bad behaviors." The study concluded that total relief "requires people to fully come clean."[4]

Psychologists are also discovering a wealth of data from our prison systems: "…inmates who tend to feel guilty for the harm they caused beat the statistical odds and stay out of trouble." This study ended with affirming this

---

2. Charles Hackney, *Positive Psychology in Christian Perspective: Foundations, Concepts, and Applications* (Downers Grove, IL: InterVarsity Press, 2021), 6.

3. Levi R. Baker, James K. McNulty, and Nickola C. Overall, "When Negative Emotions Benefit Close Relationships," in *The Positive Side of Negative Emotions* (New York, NY: Guilford Publications, 2014), 112.

4. E. Peer, S. Shalvi, and A. Acquisti, "'I Cheated, but Only a Little': Partial Confessions to Unethical Behavior," *Journal of Personality and Social Psychology* 106, no. 2 (2014): 215.

notion of guilt being good: "Guilt adds to our moral fiber, motivating us to be more socially sensitive and caring citizens than we might be otherwise...."[5]

It's astonishing to me that the very thing so many of us have perfected, that is, thinking we're protecting ourselves by never admitting any wrongdoing in the first place, is the same thing getting in the way of so much human flourishing that God longs for us to experience. We've only scratched the surface of what PP has to reveal about God's invitation to all of us—His invitation into a more abundant life through the daily habit of repentant living. It's one thing to get excited about the possibilities a psychological study reveals. It's quite another thing to actually live repentance out and experience God's promised hope firsthand.

Journal Prompt

- The Path to Flourishing: On the scale of -10 to +10 below, indicate where you feel you are in your relationship with God today? Negative numbers represent feeling distant or stuck, zero represents "neutral," and positive numbers reflect a process of flourishing in your faith. What has contributed to where you are on the scale, and what's one step you can take to move closer to +10 this week?

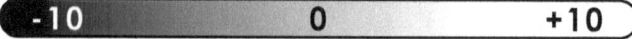

-10   0   +10

---

5. Todd Kashdan and Robert Biswas-Diener, *The Upside of Your Dark Side* (New York, NY: Plume, 2015), 82.

CHAPTER 4 | REPENTANCE MADE ME WHO I AM

Like you, I've faced real struggles, sins, and moments requiring repentance. One experience transformed my faith, reshaped my relationships, and reignited my passion for ministry. As I share my story, I hope it encourages you to think about how God might call you to experience that same freedom and renewal.

My Story

God's promise of abundant life through repentant living came out of a season when my life was falling apart. My wife and I, with our young family, had just begun what we hoped would be a lifelong career in church planting among a Muslim people group. After years of training, seminary, and language school, we were finally living our calling.

Serving in a rural area, we were settling in—learning the language, adapting to culture, building friendships, and sharing Jesus. Then, red flags appeared in our team leader's life. Soon, these red flags became blatant sins and indiscretions directly against me, my wife, and our entire family. We were heartbroken. Striving to follow Jesus' plan in Matthew 18 for conflict among believers, we initially went to our team leader to express our hurt and frustrations. That went nowhere. So, our area supervisor began mediation sessions with us.

As part of these mediation sessions, the area supervisor assigned us a worksheet with several questions. These questions were designed to have us separately reflect, write down our responses, and bring them to our next session to be ready to share. One question was, "Are there any sins you need to confess and ask forgiveness for?" Honestly, I felt insulted that I even had to reflect on such a question. I was the one who had been sinned against! Our team leader was the one who started this conflict and needed to confess and ask forgiveness from me! All of these problems I had been experiencing, all these troubles, all these feelings of negativity and despair I had been going through as I watched our entire life of ministry fall apart were surely all his fault, right?!

[Before I continue, let me address a possible concern you may have as you read. What I'm about to share has nothing to do with victim blaming. The sins

15

our team leader committed against us were inexcusable, and we were subject to a terrible time in our lives because of his indiscretions and no one else. Okay, back to my story…]

That night, frustrated by the assignment, I felt something stir—the Spirit of God convicting my heart. At that dining table, I saw my sin—hatred toward this man. No matter his actions, nothing justified my loathing. Yes, I did have sins; I needed to confess them to him and ask for forgiveness. I hated him, and there was nothing remotely Christlike about that hate. Our team leader's sins had a significant impact on the misery I was experiencing in those days, but something else contributed to my misery: my own unrepentant and hateful heart.

The next day, our final mediation session took place, and our area leader asked if anyone wanted to share their reflections on the homework. I volunteered to go first. I took out my paper, looked our team leader in the eyes, and, with genuinely heartfelt words, confessed my sin before him and asked for his forgiveness. I don't know if he ever did forgive me, but I sleep just fine at night with the assurance that God has forgiven me, and I still lament that I allowed such hatred to infect my heart in that season.

And it was amazing how quickly that healing began, starting at the very moment of confessing to my team leader. How could I tell God was already at work healing through my experience of good guilt? Well, right after I shared my confession, our area supervisor looked at our team leader and asked if he was ready to share, to which he responded, "No, because I have nothing to confess, and I'll make sure every other team of missionaries knows never to ask you on their team." And he just sat there, staring right at me.

His lack of remorse should have enraged me. His refusal to repent, his threats—everything should have pushed me over the edge. All of that should have happened, and it would have if I had not walked through my own experience of good guilt. God worked through my journey of self-examination, honest reflection, and repenting of my hate to free me in that very moment. God freed me to sit there and hear the hurtful things being said, but to be still in the peace of God, a peace I know only came because I had repented, turned more toward Him and further away from my hate, and in doing so knew joyful obedience before the Lord more than ever before.

I wish I could say the story ended the way my wife and I wanted it to. I wish I could say we are still overseas sharing Jesus with Muslims, but we're not. Over the next few weeks, our team leader followed through on his threat to put a bad taste in the mouths of other missionary teams regarding me and my family. Not a single other team invited us to join their missionary efforts. We became jobless overnight, and we had to return to the U.S.

Lesson Learned. Life Changed.

There is no doubt that God called our family to minister overseas; however, one individual's unrepentant sin brought an unnecessary end to that God-given chapter of our lives. In that situation, the best action our team leader could have taken for us, for the Muslims we were ministering to, and for himself was to offer a life of holiness to the Lord through repentance. That did not happen, and good ministry came to an end.

The best action I could have taken was the humbling of my own heart. I thank God that this was the conviction He struck me with that night while looking at our area supervisor's homework. That moment taught me my greatest lesson: the best thing I can do—for myself, my family, my church—is live a life of continual repentance, turning to God for renewal and sharing His hope with others. God redeemed an awful situation that Satan intended for evil, but God used for good! And now I'm here, sharing my passion for repentance with you. This is not just an abstract notion for me. This is a reality that has transformed my life. I could still be bitter for a dream lost, but I'm not. I love life! I am filled with joy! And I know it's all because our God is a God who keeps His promise that when we confess our sins and repent before Him, He is quick to forgive and to fill us with joyful obedience.

More than an Idea

Repentance isn't just an idea—it's how God restores and rewires us. My story is one example of how turning back to Him brings freedom, peace, and renewed purpose. As we close Part I, I hope you see repentance as powerful, not burdensome—a gift that brings life where sin once brought destruction. In Part II, we'll examine exactly how repentance works, not just why it's necessary, but why it changes us. If repentance has the power to transform our lives, then indeed it's worth leaning into with courage and trust.

Journal Prompt

- **Reflect on God's Conviction:** Recall a time God revealed a need for repentance in your life, despite feeling wronged by others. How did you respond, and what did you learn about His ability to offer peace and freedom through repentance? If not, is there an area where God invites you to repent now?

Part I Check-In

Here, at the end of Part I, take a moment to reflect on where you are in your walk with God this week. Using the scale below, mark where you honestly find yourself:

-10 (Distant, burdened by guilt) to +10 (Free, joyful in repentance)

- Where do you land this week and why?
- If you feel distant from God, is there unacknowledged guilt weighing on you? What step of repentance might bring healing and renewal?
- If you desire to grow but feel stuck, what fears or hesitations hold you back? How might embracing repentance as a gift— not a burden—help?
- If you've experienced renewal, what led you there? How can you continue to walk in the joy and freedom of repentance?

Let this be a moment of honest reflection. God's grace meets us wherever we are, but He never leaves us there.

Part II

THE PARADOX
(CHAPTERS 5-8)

CHAPTER 5 | THE PARADOX OF CONFESSION

We often think holiness means having nothing to confess, but true holiness starts with recognizing our unworthiness before God. Though counterintuitive, moving forward in Christ begins by looking back at our own sins. Thomas Oden put it this way:

> The further one walks in the way of holiness, the more deeply one is aware of one's sin. It is a paradox of sin and grace, that those who turn out to be most keenly aware of their inadequacy are walking, breathing saints. Those least aware of their sin are the most distant from repentance. Repentance continues throughout the Christian life.[1]

Fifty years before the 2023 Asbury Outpouring, revival broke out in Wilmore in the 1970s—again sparked by repentance. A single student's confession in a routine chapel service ignited 185 hours of worship. And repentance didn't end with just that one student's testimony; it continued from student to student, with one recording in their private journal at hour twenty-six that the chapel altar is "flooded with souls… Deep Repentance."[2] This pattern of deep repentance and a hunger for God set the stage for an outpouring of His Spirit, demonstrating that revival is always preceded by hearts willing to be broken, and revival continues not as people have less and less to confess but as more and more people are drawn to confess before the Lord.

Confessing Sin to Become Sinless

We all have a sin problem—individually, collectively, and globally. The same was true for a congregation 2,000 years ago; they didn't think they had a sin problem at all. That's why 1 John begins with a strong warning.

---

1. Thomas Oden, *John Wesley's Teachings, Volume 2: Christ and Salvation* (Grand Rapids: Zondervan, 2012), 272–73.

2. Robert Coleman, ed., *One Divine Moment: The Account of the Asbury Revival of 1970* (Old Tappan, NJ: Fleming H. Revell Company, 1970), 27–43.

There were many other problems going on with the congregation 1 John was addressing, including a distorted view of who Jesus was and is. But their misunderstanding of sin was so great that their pastor didn't waste any time in addressing the issue. His congregation essentially believed something that might sound familiar to us wrestling with the shallow faith that we sometimes encounter in American Christianity—they genuinely felt that they didn't have to deal with this whole "sin" or "repentance" thing anymore because they were already good to go. They said the prayer, they had been baptized, they were part of the church, and they were in great condition, right? Why confess anymore? Why repent? To which their pastor responded: "If we say that we have no sin, we deceive ourselves, and the truth is not in us... If we say that we have not sinned, we make [God] a liar, and his word is not in us" (1 John 1:8, 10). We may nod our heads in agreement with these statements, especially when thinking about those who aren't yet saved. But that's not who 1 John is written to. Like the entirety of the Bible, these words aren't written to those who don't believe; they're written to those who do.

Consider the beloved parable of the prodigal son from Luke 15. This story is often preached as a call to first-time faith, and it can be faithfully read, taught, and preached that way, but I've come to see it another light as well. Remember, the prodigal wasn't a stranger to his father. He already belonged to the family and had his inheritance. But that didn't make repentance unnecessary to his story. Repentance was essential.

It wasn't enough that the prodigal was still legally part of the family, even though he was miles away, having squandered everything, penniless and starving. It wasn't enough for him, and it's not enough for us to say, "I'm good to go, I'm already in with Jesus!" This is why the pastor's warning in 1 John is so stark: if we say we don't sin, we deceive ourselves and make a liar out of God!

So, if we who are already in Christ still sin and find that parts of our lives are miles away from the Father's house, like the prodigal, what's the answer? Well, we do what the son did; we make a change. We turn away from the path of more separation from our Father, and we start taking step after step closer to home. Each repentant step the prodigal took on his way home was a confession, one after the other, confessing that he can't do this on his own and that he needs the love of his father. And that's exactly what he received! Just as the pastor of 1 John promised, "If we confess our sins, he who is faithful and just will forgive us our sins and cleanse us from all unrighteousness" (1 John 1:9).

Like the prodigal son, the congregation at the center of the Hebrides Revival, or those at the Asbury outpouring, didn't just pray for others to repent, they recognized their own need for repentance and took steps toward God.

They took those steps, and God embraced them for it just as He promised He would! To walk in the light of Christ is not to claim perfection but to admit imperfection, trusting God's faithfulness to meet us on the path of repentance with grace and renewal, just as the prodigal son did.

A Clear Conviction of Sin

Go back through 2,000 years of church history, and you will find movement after movement illustrating everything we've been learning together in this book. For instance, Methodist founder John Wesley preached that believers must maintain a "clear conviction of the sin remaining" even after coming to faith.[3] He would also preach that "the whole body of ancient Christians" agrees that "even believers in Christ...have need to 'wrestle with flesh and blood'"; that is, we in Christ must be convinced that sin is still very real and present in our lives.[4]

It feels paradoxical. Why dwell on our sin? We assume confession is painful, yet ignoring it leads to misery. But all this time, under our noses, we've become miserable; as one Methodist theologian said, the longer we go without understanding the critical importance of repentance in our lives, the more we experience spiritual sluggishness and shipwreck.[5] Remember the promise of 1 John 1:9: "If we confess our sins, he who is faithful and just will forgive us our sins and cleanse us from all unrighteousness." That is the hope and promise of God for us. What would happen if we actually trusted that promise?

John Wesley never wavered from this call to believers in Christ to live a life of repentance. It's well known that he never stopped preaching repentance to nonbelievers, but he also kept at the forefront of his life the mission to ensure that those who currently rest in salvation's arms continue to dive even deeper into the embrace of the Father with each passing day. As we'll see later on, this movement of Methodism caught fire through day-to-day Christians committed to regular spiritual practices, many of which were purposefully repentant. Early Methodists never acted as if they were sinless. Early Methodists never claimed they had no need to repent any longer. No, they had a clear conviction of sin. They made sure to experience that conviction, that good

---

3. John Wesley, "The Scripture Way of Salvation," in *The Sermons of John Wesley: A Collection for the Christian Journey*, ed. Kenneth J. Collins and Jason E. Vickers (Nashville, TN: Abingdon Press, 2013), 587.

4. John Wesley, "On Sin in Believers," in *The Sermons of John Wesley: A Collection for the Christian Journey*, ed. Kenneth J. Collins and Jason E. Vickers (Nashville, TN: Abingdon Press, 2013), 560.

5. Owen Alderfer, "John Wesley on Aspects of Christian Experience After Justification," *The Asbury Journal 18, no. 2* (January 1, 1964): 9, https://doi.org/10.7252/Journal.01.1964Jun.02.

guilt, in their hearts, and God birthed a worldwide movement still blessing the world today because of it.

First Steps

It's one thing to *read* about repentance—it's another to *live* it. And starting is simple. Right now, you can experience this paradox firsthand: true abundance comes through humble self-examination. By reflecting on these words, you've already begun to embrace good guilt. I wonder... how has God already shown you His hope and promise by turning toward good guilt instead of hiding from it?

There will be more information to follow about ways you and your church can practically practice repentant living as individuals and as a church, but for now, I want to challenge you to do just one thing. Begin your day and end your night with this simple prayer: "Lord Jesus Christ, have mercy on me, for I have sinned." That's it. Add that prayer at the beginning and end of your day and see what God does with it!

Even if no specific sins come to mind, pray anyway. Don't fall into the trap of thinking, "We've got nothing to confess!" Even if you feel that way, there may still be some unknowing sin against God's will. You might not recognize it, but God does, and He longs to offer you forgiveness. Often, it's in praying this prayer that I recall certain sins, and it grieves me. I embrace this guilt, give my confessions to God, and trust that all my sins are washed away by the blood of the lamb. I believe that through confession, my heavenly Father welcomes me deeper into His home than before I prayed.

As you begin to embrace this practice of daily repentance, remember that every step taken in confession brings you closer to God's heart. Repentance is not about wallowing in guilt but walking in grace, knowing that God meets us in our humility with abundant mercy and love. By turning toward Him with honest confessions, we not only find personal renewal but also prepare the way for His Spirit to move powerfully in our lives and communities.

Journal Prompt

- **Reflect on Your Journey Home:** Reflect on where you have strayed from God, relying on yourself. Like the prodigal son, what does "turning back" mean for you? Write down one or two steps of repentance this week, trusting in God's love and grace on your journey home.

CHAPTER 6 | WHY CONFESSION WORKS

Maybe you're almost convinced about repentance, but you need to know *how* it works. I get it. I, too, need to understand the mechanics before I commit to something.

Our Advocate and Atoning Sacrifice

The early church reading 1 John wasn't just told confession brings hope; they were shown how God works through it: "…if anybody does sin, we have an advocate with the Father—Jesus Christ, the Righteous One. He is the atoning sacrifice for our sins…" (1 John 2:1b–2a NIV). Remember, this church is at a crisis point. They've entirely neglected even acknowledging the power of sin to destroy their lives. The author longs to convince them to change their ways, so he rests his entire argument on Christ's presence in this world, his advocacy for us before the Father, and his sacrificial death on the cross.

We rarely use "advocate" today, but its meaning helps us grasp Jesus' role. Maybe you picture a lawyer defending a client or a healthcare advocate ensuring proper care. I know when my wife and I are struggling with health issues, we often want and need the other with us when we're in doctor's appointments to help advocate for us—to be on our side and help us get the best possible care. Those illustrations barely scratch the surface of Jesus' advocacy for us, but the idea is the same: he is there to *help us.*

We fear confession because we fear abandonment.

We fear confession because we fear abandonment. We already feel isolated, convinced that if others knew our failures, they'd leave us. So, what do we do? We hide that thing deep inside, unconfessed. But 1 John assures us that confession doesn't lead to abandonment but to Jesus, our ever-present helper. I love how Raymond Brown, an expert on 1 John, so dramatically describes Jesus' help when he says that Christ is our "advocate in the Father's presence *against a satan who would claim sinners for his own.*"[1]

The Greek word *halismos*, translated as "atoning sacrifice" or "expiation," appears only once in scripture, in 1 John 2:2. The Holy Spirit reserved this Greek word just for this moment to help Christians 2,000 years ago and Christians today understand how it is that God can turn something like guilt into something good for us and can heal, cleanse, and bring new life to our lives through willingly experiencing that guilt through repentant confession. Since this is the only time this word is used in scripture, it is extraordinarily difficult to translate into a single English word, so I'll let someone much brighter than me do that for us: *halismos* conveys ideas of "blood, cleansing, the innocent victim, and the idea that the one who atones is himself in heaven continuing to cleanse, thus offering a basis of confidence for sinners."[2]

Books could be written on Jesus as our *halismos*, but simply put, by His blood, He brings complete cleansing. And just as important is the promise that Jesus' sacrifice on the cross was not only some past event that only atoned for our sins the moment we became Christians. Jesus was not just our *halismos* on the cross 2,000 years ago or just our *halismos* when we initially gave our lives to Christ. The role of *halismos* is not trapped in the past; it is a very real and present role of Christ for the very real and present sins still active in our lives today. Jesus is not just the atoning sacrifice to get you into heaven; he continues to be the atoning sacrifice, sitting at the right hand of God, advocating for you as he holds back Satan from your life, and getting heaven—his holiness—into your life today! Another New Testament scholar, Judith Lieu, beautifully summarizes this reality in this way: "This is where Jesus belongs; not to the past... but as the continuing means of maintaining and restoring fellowship, if only those who would claim it also acknowledge their need."[3]

Consider the prodigal son story and its relevance today; it's not only about how you were embraced by God's love as a Christian. Recognize that there are still areas in your life where you are wandering far from the Father's house of grace and love. Salvation didn't simply happen the day you came to faith in Jesus; salvation *began*, and the process of salvation

---

1. Raymond E. Brown, *The Epistles of John* (Garden City, NY: Doubleday & Company, Inc., 1982), 242. Emphasis added.

2. Rudolf Schnackenburg, *The Johannine Epistles*, trans. Reginald Fuller and Ilse Fuller (New York, NY: The Crossroads Publishing Company, 1992), 88.

3. Judith Lieu, *I, II, & III John: A Commentary*, The New Testament Library (Louisville, KY: Westminster John Knox Press, 2008), 67.

continues in your life today. The reason the Father is waiting for you at the gates of the house, the reason you can trust that the Father absolutely will welcome you home is because our great helper, Jesus Christ, has fought for, and is still fighting for you against the ways of Satan to bring you home. All you need to do is keep taking those steps of confession, that inch-by-inch journey of repentance into your Father's arms. Confession isn't about convincing God to forgive us. The Father has already planned to welcome you *fully* home. Repentant living is about more fully receiving the forgiveness and the welcome home He's already made available through Christ.

Putting the Mechanics to Work

Jesus wasn't just our *halismos* 2,000 years ago—He is today, helping us grow closer to the Father. So, let's practice what we've learned. Take a deep breath, and for the next 10–15 minutes or so, be still and silent as you work through these steps, and trust in Jesus, your "advocate" and "atoning sacrifice."

1. **Recognize Sin:** Reflect on your life and identify areas where you've strayed from God's will. Consider specific actions, thoughts, or attitudes that have led you away from Him.

   - *Image*: Picture the prodigal son in the far country, realizing he is starving while his father's house overflows with abundance. His moment of clarity starts the journey home.

   - *Practical Tip*: Pray, "Lord, help me see where I have wandered from You today."

2. **Name the Sin:** Be specific about what you confess. Generalities like "I made mistakes" are ok if you genuinely can't think of anything but be wary of using general phrases as a crutch to keep you from fully being honest before the Lord. Honesty breaks the cycle of avoiding good guilt.

   - *Image*: Picture the prodigal son rehearsing his confession on his way home: "Father, I have sinned against heaven and you." The clarity of his words reflects the clarity of his heart.

   - *Practical Tip*: Speak or write plainly to God: "I spoke harshly today," or "I was jealous of a friend's success."

29

3. **Ask for and Receive Grace:** Trust that God's forgiveness is already available through Jesus. Confession is your way of receiving the grace Jesus freely gives. Be open to God's hope and promises pouring into your life as He works through your good guilt to bring renewal.

   ○ *Image*: Picture Jesus standing as your advocate before the Father, like a defender in court, proclaiming that his sacrifice covers every sin.

   ○ *Practical Tip*: Pray, "Lord Jesus Christ, thank you for being my Advocate and Atoning Sacrifice. I receive your forgiveness today."

4. **Repeat Regularly:** Confession is an ongoing practice. Just as the prodigal son's journey home was step-by-step, repentance is a continual return to the Father.

   ○ *Image*: Imagine the prodigal walking toward the father's house, one step at a time, each step bringing him closer to restoration.

   ○ *Practical Tip*: Begin and end each day with a prayer of confession, asking God to reveal and heal what separates you from Him.

"But You Don't Know What I've Done"

There's one final pushback to all of this: the lie that God's grace is for others but not for you. That your sins are too great. But 1 John 2:2 makes clear Jesus' atonement isn't just for you; it's for the "sins of the whole world." Jesus looks at us and our belief that our sins are too great and essentially says, "Hold my beer" (or "Hold my chalice of wine" for our first-century Middle Eastern Jesus). He tells us to "hold tight and watch this!" as he shows us he can forgive even the worst of our sins because he can do that and even more for the sins of the whole world. Nothing, absolutely nothing, can hold Jesus back from being your helper and atoning sacrifice, not even you! Trust his invitation into good guilt—where more of your heart and soul find their way home.

Journal Prompt

- **Reflect on Jesus as Your Advocate:** Imagine Jesus before the Father, defending you against Satan's claim. How does this alter your perspective on confession and God's forgiveness? Identify one area in your life where you need to trust Jesus as your Advocate and seek His grace instead of fearing condemnation.

CHAPTER 7 | GOOD FOR THE BRAIN...AND THE SOUL!

One more paradox of good guilt that I haven't touched on yet: the 1 John congregation thought they had no need for confession, yet their pastor longed for them to *truly* be free from sin. Their pastor states his desire for the congregation: "I am writing these things to you so that you may not sin" (1 Jn 2:1). Out of all of this section of 1 John we are exploring, this may be the most important verse to me personally because it's so filled with hope!

Like you, I don't want repentance to be about self-loathing. I need hope— I need this journey to be worth it. I need there to be an end goal in mind. Well, here it is: *so that I may not sin*! It sounds so good that it sounds impossible. But there it is. Plain as day. Clear as crystal—*so that you may not sin*.

Good guilt is not something we experience over and over with no promise of change. Good guilt, when experienced the way God designed it, has a massive, huge, earth-shattering goal at the end of it: the promise that we can not only be saved from the *condemnation* of sin, but also from the *power* of sin. What I mean is we have a savior, Jesus Christ, who not only saves us into the eternal arms of God but also a savior who frees us from the day-to-day grind of sin in our Sunday through Saturday lives. Good guilt isn't just a temporary fix on this or that sin. Through honest, self-examining, regular repentance before the Lord, God says, "Let's fix this together!" And He wants to fix it for good! Good guilt has a good, no, a *great* goal—that we would live into the very promise of God that He wants to make us holy as He is holy. To borrow from the author of 1 John, *I'm writing to you so that you may not sin*. I'm writing to you so that you can experience the abundant life of Christ now. I'm writing to you with faith and confidence that what Jesus has promised, a life of holiness here and now, he will perform in our lives if we are turning to him. Imagine if we walked through life with hope that such a thing is possible. And it's not just a hope we can only look forward to. This newness of life is a reality that can absolutely be expected as we step into good guilt.

Moving to Positive Ten

As I explained before, most psychology has focused on moving people from -10 to 0, from misery to survival. How much of Christian ministry has done the same, just getting people in the door? Positive Psychology's goal of moving people from surviving to flourishing is laudable, but is it possible? The data shows that it is and that the human act of owning up to mistakes plays a key role in that flourishing.

Positive Psychologist Charles Hackney reminds us that flourishing does not happen "by cutting negative experiences out of our lives and focusing exclusively on enhancing cheerfulness."[1] Or, to echo warnings from 1 John, human flourishing doesn't happen by denying, covering up, or ignoring the fact that we sin. Human flourishing comes by adopting a spiritual value that is also a key value within PP—humility. This type of humility is specifically the humility needed to look beyond self-comfort, pleasure, and ease and instead be willing to wallow through the mud of our own souls for a bit to see what's really in there. Once we humble ourselves enough to experience some of this good guilt over what we've done, the evidence is impressive. Research links anxiety, depression, and even heart disease to self-centeredness. The more we ignore our faults, the worse we feel.

Good guilt is the Holy Spirit's tool to break the self-destructive cycle that science is now confirming. Guilt is our God-created conscience calling us back into alignment with what God knows is good and true for our lives. Being humble and honest about our lives, even the most difficult parts of our lives, and acknowledging our mistakes can help us "gain emotional agility [and] the ability to use the full palette of emotional experiences."[2] And this process of "unselving" our lives from our sinful propensity for comfort and ease "may have significant psychological and physical benefits."[3]

There's even evidence that verbalizing our mistakes and letting our confessions flow over our vocal cords and out of our mouths can help us flourish: "Putting upsetting experiences into words allows people to stop inhibiting their thoughts and feelings, and to organize their thoughts and perhaps find meaning."[4] Consider the emotional clarity of the prodigal son when he finally gave in to the Spirit's prompting of guilt in his life, emotional clarity that the

---

1. Hackney, *Positive Psychology in Christian Perspective: Foundations, Concepts, and Applications*, 238.

2. Kashdan and Biswas-Diener, *The Upside of Your Dark Side*, 93.

3. June P. Tangney, "Humility," in *Handbook of Positive Psychology*, ed. S. J. Lopez and C. R. Snyder (New York, NY: Oxford University Press, 2002), 416.

4. Kate G. Niederhoffer and James W. Pennebaker, "Sharing One's Story: On the Benefits of Writing or Talking About Emotional Experience," in *Handbook of Positive Psychology*, ed. S. J. Lopez and C. R. Snyder (New York, NY: Oxford University Press, 2002), 581.

son even verbalized: "But when he came to himself he said… 'I will get up and go to my father, and I will say to him, "Father, I have sinned…"'" So he set off and went to his father" (Luke 15:17–20). The prodigal wasn't just going from negative ten to zero; the son started his journey to a flourishing positive ten because instead of hiding from his guilt, he embraced it, he verbalized it, and he actively stepped into it as a bridge to a wholeness unlike anything he had yet experienced.

The Guilt that Heals… and Heals… and Heals…

One repentant heart can transform a community. Three hundred years ago, a refugee group called the Moravians found healing on the land of Count Nicholas von Zinzendorf, a man devoted to holiness. He not only exemplified closeness with Jesus in his compassion for the Moravians, but he displayed a clarity of understanding around repentance as well. Over time, the Moravians fell into bitter conflict, each convinced they were right.

Zinzendorf called them to repentance and prayer. After three days, revival broke out at a communion service. Pastor Mark Nysewande describes the healed Moravians at the end of those three days as a people "being transformed from religious bickering to unity and joy…."[5] And this joy wasn't just for the Moravians but would change the religious landscape of the entire globe for the next three centuries!

Zinzendorf was a man who didn't push things down, hide mistakes, or ignore sin. He practiced self-examination daily. He was known to publicly confess any known sin in his life. He was a deeply holy man because he was a profoundly repentant man. It wasn't surprising to anyone that he also called the bickering Moravians to the same practice. And it likely wasn't surprising to Zinzendorf that such repentance brought healing to that community. However, what may have been surprising is just how far that healing reached and is still reaching.

If you're Methodist, Wesleyan, or part of a holiness movement, your heritage of faith traces back to the Moravian Revival. Many Christian traditions were shaped by their repentance and renewal. Those three days of repentant and unifying prayer turned into one hundred years of revival. Yes, a one-hundred-year prayer movement began that would send out hundreds of missionaries, inspire countless other revivals, and birth many other Christian movements worldwide.

One such mission effort from these Moravians would go to London. They would establish a regular Bible study in a home off of one of the city's main streets, Aldersgate Street, to be exact. One day, an invitation was made to a

---

5. Nysewander, *Revival Rising*, 109.

young English priest named John Wesley to come and join this study. He didn't want to go, but the Holy Spirit did something that day. The Spirit continued the ministry of healing, which had begun on Zinzendorf's land a decade earlier, in one man's heart that night. Wesley wrote in his journal that he went quite "unwillingly" to this Bible study. Still, the moment the study began, God's healing caught hold of Wesley's soul, "strangely warmed" his heart, and a movement of God called Methodism began that so many others and I around the world are a part of, and through which so many still experience God's healing touch. All because Zinzendorf led a repentant life of holiness unto God.

Does God want you to experience a flourishing life at a positive ten? Absolutely! But don't limit God to work through the power of good guilt just in your own life. God can flourish in your life and the lives of countless others through your own simple repentant living before the Lord. Count Nicholas von Zinzendorf surely experienced healing in his own life through repentant living. He shared the gift of good guilt with the Moravians, calling them to prayer. And their healing spilled over into the entire world! Jesus can heal bodies, minds, and souls through the conviction of sin and the repentant heart, and he can do so in multitudes.

From Survival to Flourishing

Good guilt isn't just about survival—it's about flourishing. Scripture and psychology agree: confession and humility bring healing, growth, and joy. What if we, like the prodigal son, turned homeward in repentance? What if, like Zinzendorf, our humility sparked revival? This is the promise of good guilt: a healing that doesn't just mend what is broken but breathes new life into weary souls. In embracing this truth, we step toward God's invitation to be forgiven and set free— to live abundantly, thrive, and bring others into the freedom of God's love.

Journal Prompt

- **Reflect on Hope and Flourishing:** Reflect on 1 John 2:1, which states, "I am writing these things to you so that you may not sin." How does this promise offer hope in your repentance journey? Identify one area where you feel stuck in unhealthy patterns. How can embracing "good guilt" and confessing to God help you move from merely surviving to truly flourishing?

CHAPTER 8 | BREAKING BREAD.
BREAKING CHAINS!

I love when science confirms what scripture already reveals about God's grace. My hope in forgiveness is fully rooted in the Gospel, but it's encouraging to see PP affirm the power of confession.

A recent study identified key steps in rituals that help individuals and communities move through guilt toward renewal. For such practices to be effective, they argued, they must include: "(a) a recognition of personal transgressions; (b) reparations for the misdeeds; and (c) a 'cleaning of the slate,' accompanied by divine acceptance, forgiveness, and reconciliation."[1] They went on to conclude that when an individual walks through such steps, there is a positive correlation between the person's admission of guilt and their improved quality of life, even to the point of enhancing the confessor's "physical health over the long run."[2] I wonder... Has God blessed us with such a ritual to practice in our own lives of faith to help us experience together the good guilt that leads to newness of life?

A "Means of Grace" as a Means to Flourishing

In Methodism, "means of grace" are practices through which we encounter God's presence. While God works in countless ways, the church recognizes specific methods, including worship, prayer, service, and the sacraments. Bible study and regular worship with other Christians are means of grace. Feeding the hungry and visiting the poor and sick are means of grace. Prayer and fasting are means of grace. And, of course, our two sacraments, baptism and communion, are means of grace, and impactful ones at that!

---

1. Kenneth I Pargament and Annette Mahoney, "Spirituality: Discovering and Conserving the Sacred," in *Handbook of Positive Psychology*, ed. C. R. Snyder and S. J. Lopez (New York, NY: Oxford University Press, 2002), 652.

2. Pargament and Mahoney, "Spirituality: Discovering and Conserving the Sacred," 653.

As a pastor, I see how baptism and communion align with PP's findings on confession and renewal. And, as I seek to find ways to help my congregation walk closer with Christ week after week, I am intrigued by what God can do through the regular practice of communion to help Christ's followers experience good guilt and the flourishing that God has promised and data from PP has proven.

As we'll explore later, Methodist founder John Wesley argued that a repentant heart was the only attribute necessary to feast at the communion table. This repentant posture is the "recognition of personal transgressions" required in the above-mentioned ritual formula.

The "reparations for misdeeds" in the PP formula also appear in communion. Congregants approach the table as living sacrifices, understanding that the broken bread and the cup represent the presence of the sacrificed Christ, providing necessary reparations for their sins. The Christian does not make these reparations; grace is granted through God's work in Christ.

Then, in communion, there should always be absolution, a pardon and assurance from the pastor by which the congregants hear the reassuring words of Christ's cleansing, which align with what PP says is needed for a human to effectively walk through good guilt into a flourishing life. Again, in our Christian ritual of communion, it is not the individual who does the cleansing but God; nonetheless, the necessary component of the "cleaning of the slate" from the ritual formula mentioned above is powerfully present.

How PP confirms what is experienced in Holy Communion	
PP Theory on Effective Ritual Practice	Sacrament of Holy Communion in Methodism
A recognition of personal transgressions	The only requirement to come to the communion table is a repentant heart.
Reparations for misdeeds	Reparations are sufficiently made by the body and blood of Jesus Christ.
A cleaning of the slate	Confession as part of communion comes with assurance of pardon.

Hope For Grace

This isn't just theory—I've seen it firsthand. During my five years pastoring Grace Methodist Church in Alamogordo, NM, weekly confession through communion transformed the congregation's hope. Week after week, the congregation practiced repentance as they confessed their sins openly, communally, and publicly. This weekly confession didn't bog them down with shame, it didn't burden them with despair, and it didn't bring a dark cloud over them. Through their regular experience of good guilt in the context of weekly communion, God brought them hope as they took seriously scripture's command to examine themselves (1 Corinthians 11:28) before feasting at the Lord's table.

When I first arrived at Grace Methodist, they were in year twenty of a consistent pattern of numerical decline or plateau. Their last significant year of new growth in that church was in the late 1990s. One member told me that the past two decades had been the "graying of Grace," referring to the graying of people's heads in the pews. Finding hope in the congregation was hard when I got there. However, they were already (and thankfully) practicing weekly communion due to the diligent pastoring of my predecessor. So, we leaned into that practice, and we leaned into it hard! I couldn't shake this hunch that regular repentance before the Lord as a single church body, week after week, could bring this church out of its funk. What a blessing it was to discover that's exactly what God longed to do, and would do, during my tenure there!

Like many century-old churches, Grace Methodist faced decline, and much blame was cast elsewhere. Our fallen human instinct is to avoid responsibility and blame others. It's understandably hard for churches to admit their own role in their decline. This was the case at Grace Methodist as well. When asked about who/what was most to blame for the past couple decades of decline, the predominant response was typically to blame influences outside church walls that were beyond their control or to blame denominational leaders. (In Methodism, that typically means Bishops and/or District Superintendents.) This information isn't just anecdotal. I was so curious about this notion of good guilt, especially as experienced through holy communion, that I spent three years of doctoral work trying to wrap my head (and heart) around all that God could do through it at the local church level. After an intentional season of walking congregants through these ideas and repentant practices, with my own eyes, I saw the power of God bring hope into a congregation when they embraced good guilt.

Of the congregants I observed in my doctoral work (through self-guided journal entries and surveys), I was blessed to witness the power of good guilt to bring newness of life to individuals and a congregation. Congregants shifted dramatically from blaming outside influences and denominational leaders for their decline to realizing that they themselves had likely played a significant role in the past twenty years of decline. For example, there was a 25% *decrease* in the congregants' propensity to blame Bishops or District Superintendents for all that had happened over two decades. If you know anything about

Methodists, this is a huge shift. These denominational leaders are easy fodder for blame. For a congregation to openly acknowledge that they themselves may have contributed to ministry failures or mistakes is quite something!

And these self-admissions weren't just generic expressions of abstract guilt. These were spoken/written confessions that owned up to their contribution to ministry decline. One congregant shared, "We have not placed God first in our hearts, that we have failed to listen to God." Another expressed guilt that "we have failed our children/youth by not showing Christ's love [to them]." One confessed that "we are not always open to change, or open to listening to someone's opinions and ideas," while another admitted to an "unwillingness to change." I could go on and on regarding how this congregation began to express genuine, heartfelt repentance before the Lord. And none of this happened in a vacuum, but it was all couched in the means of grace of holy communion. Each time the bread of Christ was shared, and the cup of salvation was offered, congregants were asked and expected to practice confession and repentance. Each time they came to the table, they heard God's absolute promise of forgiveness from me, their pastor, and they then experienced that promise of newness of life firsthand as they ate the bread and drank from the cup.

This experience of constant confession, week after week, did not leave them in gloom and doom, as is often the fear when we consider thinking about our faults, mistakes, and sins. No, this constant confession, this regular willing desire to experience good guilt, renewed new hope and promise in this church! One member acknowledged being "more joyful, more hopeful, more enthusiastic." Another realized that by stepping through the experience of good guilt, they can see "more clearly now what God has in store for our church… We could be seeding growth for growth in a church." One simply (and beautifully) summarized their aha(!) moment of realizing that in earnestly self-examining and confession sins before God, "there's just a feeling [that] there's hope."

Overall, the number of people at Grace Methodist in Alamogordo who said they were genuinely optimistic about the church's future grew by 40%! This growth in hope didn't come from any motivational speech. It didn't happen because of some new curriculum or Bible study. It didn't happen because some new pastor came in and made the congregation feel better about themselves. It came because a group of faithful followers of Jesus heard God's call to live repentant lives, so that's what they did. They courageously trusted God to walk them through a season of good guilt, and what they experienced on the other side was a newness of life and a genuine desire to be joyously obedient to whatever God was calling them to do next. They didn't hide or ignore their sin; they confessed their sin, because "he who is faithful and just will forgive us our sins and cleanse us from all unrighteousness..." for Jesus is the atoning sacrifice for sins—he is the broken bread and poured out cup; not for ours only but also for the sins of the whole world. (1 John 1:9; 2:2)

I am no longer the pastor at Grace Methodist Church, and revival hasn't broken out there yet. But even as I pastor another church, I pray for Grace Methodist daily, and I know that the first steps of revival have been laid as they have taken and continue to take the regular steps of good guilt together as a congregation.

Brokenness Faced and Hearts Renewed

Revival begins with a broken heart—not in despair, but in hope. Repentance confronts sin, not to crush us, but to free us. We've seen how confession becomes a gateway to renewal, whether at the communion table or in our daily lives. It is stepping closer to the Father's house, like the prodigal son, trusting that every faltering step is met with God's embrace.

Conviction of sin leads not to shame but to good guilt—a sorrow that transforms. This is the thread running through the examples of revival we've explored: communities and individuals willing to face their brokenness, who find not condemnation but the healing and hope of restoration. These examples remind us that repentance doesn't end with confessing sin. It opens the door to a life continually shaped by grace, a life where guilt isn't a burden to carry but a tool God uses to refine us.

Journal Prompt

- **Reflect on Your Practice of Communion:** Think back to your last communion experience. Did you approach the table with a repentant heart, fully confessing your burdens to God? If not, what might need to shift in your practice to make communion a more meaningful act of repentance and renewal? Write about how embracing confession at the table could deepen your experience of God's grace.

Part II Check-In

As we close Part II, take a moment to reflect on how confession, repentance, and God's grace are shaping your journey. Using the scale below, mark where you honestly find yourself:

-10 (Resistant, burdened by guilt) to +10 (Free, renewed through confession and grace).

-10   0   +10

- Where do you land this week and why?

- If you feel stuck in guilt or resistance, what's keeping you there? Is there a confession or step of humility you've been avoiding?

- If you long to grow but feel hesitant, what fears or doubts hold you back? How might embracing confession as a gift (not a burden) help you move forward?

- If you've experienced renewal, what brought you there? How can regular confession and repentance continue to deepen your joy?

Let this be a moment of honest reflection. Confession isn't about staying in guilt—it's about stepping into God's grace. He meets us where we are, but He invites us to go further.

Part III

GOOD GUILT VS. BAD GUILT (CHAPTERS 9–12)

CHAPTER 9 | RUN AWAY FROM SHAME

Our struggle with guilt and blame traces back to Genesis 3. When confronted, Adam took no responsibility but blamed Eve, and even God: "The woman whom you gave to be with me, she gave me fruit from the tree, and I ate" (Genesis 3:12). Not only does Adam blame Eve, but he also blames God in the process! Did you catch that? "The woman *whom you gave* to be with me." We're so good at denying our sins that we even use God Himself as a scapegoat.

Genesis 3 also reveals our tendency to embrace toxic shame instead of God's sanctifying gift of good guilt. I briefly alluded to this difference between shame and guilt in Chapter 1 in my first attempt to invite you to experience good guilt for what it is—a bridge to hope and joy—as opposed to the paralyzing effect that shame can have. Notice Adam and Eve's response when they realize their mistake of disobeying God's desires for their life together in the garden. When they heard God coming their way and with full knowledge of what they had done wrong, "…the man and his wife hid themselves from the presence of the LORD…" (Gen 3:8). They did the opposite of repentance—hiding instead of turning to God. They continued in their sin, denied their need for God, and ran away.

Then, when God catches up to them (as God always does), Adam responds with the following: "…I was afraid, because I was naked…" (Genesis 3:10). Look carefully at that verse again. Notice what Adam doesn't do. There's zero confession of the actual sin initially committed. There's no recognition that taking and eating the fruit was wrong and should never have happened. That would have been stepping into the good guilt that I believe God longed for Adam to experience then and for us to experience now. Nothing about what Adam says to God is about what he did. He didn't communicate his guilt. He only communicates his shame. He only communicates the state he found himself in: fear and nakedness. And what did he do when that was the only thing he allowed himself to experience? He hid from God. Adam was afraid and naked. The shame he felt was no one's fault but his own. But he gave in to his shame—that reality of his fear and nakedness—and hid himself from God rather than leaning into his guilt and trusting in God to forgive, embrace, and restore him.

Guilt vs. Shame

Defining shame and guilt varies across cultures and studies, but PP offers a helpful distinction. Consider this differentiation between the two: "In both cases [of guilt and shame], one acknowledges fault for a wrongdoing, but in guilt, one makes attributions about the act itself ('it was a bad thing to do'), whereas, in shame, one makes attributions about the entire self ('I'm a bad person')."[1] In Genesis 3, Adam wasn't opening himself to guilt ("taking and eating of the tree was wrong"), he was only falling into shame ("I was naked and afraid"). Sadly, many Christians today follow the same pattern as Adam—only allowing themselves to experience shame in the face of wrongdoings instead of stepping into guilt.

In the Methodist/Wesleyan tradition, we distinguish between sin in unbelievers and believers. For the unbeliever, sin is very much ingrained in that person's identity. We are indeed sinners in need of a gracious God. But for believers, Christ defines our identity. It frustrates me when Christians say, *"I'm just a sinner."* No, in Christ, you are a saint, redeemed and raised to new life! "If you confess with your lips that Jesus is Lord and believe in your heart that God raised him from the dead" (Romans 10:9), you are not a sinner. You are a saint! Yes, you are most likely a saint still struggling with sin, but you are a saint, nonetheless. To fail in recognizing this cheapens Christ's death for you and the world. Remember, he didn't just die to get you into heaven. He died to get heaven into you right here and now. Again, in Christ, you are a saint! Never forget that.

I believe this distinction between guilt and shame in the life of the Christian—that is, between identifying as a bad person (shame) versus identifying as a person who still does bad things (guilt)—helps us focus on why so many Christians still struggle to see repentance as a necessary and important thing in their life. A 2013 Barna study revealed a lack of repentant living in the lives of Christians: While 64% of self-professed American Christians claim to have confessed sin to God,[2] that leaves a large portion—close to one third—of self-professing Christians who have not taken one of the critical steps to actually be a Christian, that is, confess sin to God. That same study showed that only 3% felt they had fully surrendered to Christ. What if what many Christians hear when called to "repent" isn't heard as a call to good guilt but to toxic shame? And if they feel shame induced by calls to repent, then it is no wonder that so few Christians actively step into repentant living.

---

1. Nicole E Henniger and Christine R Harris, "Can Negative Social Emotions Have Positive Consequences?," in *The Positive Side of Negative Emotions* (New York, NY: Guilford Publications, n.d.), 81.

2. "Self-Described Christians Dominate America but Wrestle with Four Aspects of Spiritual Depth," Barna Group, September 11, 2013, https://www.barna.com/research/self-described-christians-dominate-america-but-wrestle-with-four-aspects-of-spiritual-depth/.

Hope Beyond Shame

Adam should have run toward God in his guilt, but he ran away in shame. The church must call people to repentance, not shame. Yes, we were once inherently sinful, but we are now new creations! The call to repent in our lives is equally as important as the call to repent in the lives of nonbelievers, but it is now an altogether different call. In the church, we need to call ourselves to the regular practice of repentance in order to experience the positive effects of guilt, not to shame people into thinking they're only sinners. We need to adapt our understanding of Christian repentance away from condemning the whole Christian person, which induces shame, to condemning the Christian's behavior, which induces guilt. As research confirms, "Guilt pushes us to confess, apologize, and make reparations, while shame pushes us to protect our pride and restore perceived lost status."[3]

Our fear of feeling shame keeps us from honest self-examination, so we build walls to protect our pride. But it doesn't have to be this way. Congregations far and wide need not fear such shame; they can move beyond shame and experience true hope because, in Christ, our identity is no longer found in our sins; it is found in Him! A Christian person confessing sin is not confessing that at their core they are a bad person. A Christian person confessing is embracing the reality that God has done, and continues to do, a good and gracious work in their life.

Shame leads to hiding, but guilt invites healing. The church must not only make new disciples but also guide believers beyond shame into the freedom of good guilt, which is God's gift to draw us closer to Him. Repentance, when rightly understood, is not a burden but a pathway to renewal and flourishing. As we look to Christ as the foundation of our identity, we can confront our mistakes with courage, trusting in God's grace to restore and redeem. This shift from shame to guilt paves the way for the kind of self-examination that sparks personal growth, corporate revival, and deeper intimacy with God.

Journal Prompt

- **Reflecting on Guilt vs. Shame:** Recall a time you felt wrong. Did you respond with shame ("I am bad") or guilt ("I did something bad")? Consider how to embrace guilt as a call to repentance instead of letting shame lead you to hide.

---

3. Hackney, *Positive Psychology in Christian Perspective: Foundations, Concepts, and Applications*, 20.

CHAPTER 10 | LEAN INTO GUILT

Shame makes us hide, build barriers, and protect our pride, even at the cost of denying our sins. Adam and Eve hid in fear, ashamed of their nakedness, instead of turning to the only one who could restore them. Eons later, in a first century Mediterranean church, a congregation of Adam's descendants was so fearful of being exposed before God, so afraid of experiencing shame before the Lord, that they denied their sin altogether, claiming total sinlessness, to which their pastor forcefully responded, "If we say that we have no sin, we deceive ourselves... [and] make [God] a liar, and his word is not in us" (1 John 1:8, 10).

The danger of shame over guilt is not just a psychological theory; it's biblical truth. From Genesis 3 to 1 John and all the places in between, God continually reminds us of His call on our lives to repent, not out of fear of experiencing shame, but out of hope of what the power of God can do when we lean into the Spirit's conviction of good guilt in our lives.

Good Guilt in the Scriptures

Pages and pages could be written about God's people practicing repentance because of God's conviction of good guilt. Let me barely scratch the surface of those examples by sharing a few of my favorites, all of which are portrayals not of people outside the faith repenting for the first time but of people already part of God's people—people not excused from repentance just because they're "already in," but people who deeply need to experience good guilt to live the flourishing life that God longs for them to have.

THE ISRAELITES AND THE GOLDEN CALF (EXODUS 32 & 33)

Here's a classic Sunday school story if there ever was one. Freshly freed from Egypt, the Israelites were on the path to flourishing. God had already claimed these people as His own. He put His entire reputation on the line to rescue them from Egypt. These were *His people*, and He claimed as much to Moses chapters earlier, "I have observed the misery of *my people* in Egypt…" (Exodus 3:7 CSB, emphasis added). These weren't outsiders needing to repent to get into God's good graces. They were already there. But we know how the story goes.

Like us, the Israelites still wrestled with sin despite their freedom. And in the face of sin's temptation, they built a golden calf and worshiped it. Prompted by the Spirit, Moses declared just how abhorrent such sin was in God's eyes, as all sin is. At this declaration, the Israelites felt the guilt they needed to understand the grave error of their ways. "They mourned" their actions, the text says in Exodus 33:4, and this mourning led to a difficult journey but ultimately a journey of restoration back to God. Their sin had consequences, but through repentance, they mourned, turned back to God, and continued toward the Promised Land.

ISAIAH'S VISION (ISAIAH 6)

The story of the Golden Calf is a powerful example of God's ability to restore an entire group through communal repentance. Isaiah's story is equally powerful in displaying how good guilt stirs revival in the heart of one individual. In Isaiah's first five chapters, he appears to be a faithful follower of God. From verse one of chapter one, we're told that this man has prophetic visions from God. Isaiah was already a leader among God's people, yet even he needed repentance. Even Isaiah needed to lean into the conviction of good guilt to experience even more of what God intended for him.

One day, Isaiah was caught up in a vision. In this vision, he was in the very presence of God Himself, and guilt *immediately* took hold of Isaiah's spirit. "Woe is me! I am lost, for I am a man of unclean lips…," he says in Isaiah 6:5 at the sight of God's glory. Isaiah made no excuses or attempts to hide. He admitted his unworthiness before God. He leaned into his guilt and bared it all before God. Then, something remarkable happened. God didn't turn Isaiah away. God didn't chastise or rebuke Isaiah. God didn't shame Isaiah. God cleansed him! After being touched by a lump of heavenly burning coal, he heard from the heavens these words, "Now that this has touched your lips, your guilt has departed and your sin is blotted out" (Isaiah 6:7). Only then, after Isaiah leaned into his guilt and didn't turn away from it, was Isaiah willing and able to step even more into God's call, into the newness of life and joyful obedience that only God can bring, saying, "Hear am I: send me" (Isaiah 6:8).

PETER AFTER DENYING JESUS (LUKE 22:54–62)

Now to one of the most famous New Testament failures: Peter's three-time denial of Jesus. In reality, this is what each of us do when we sin as Christians—deny to ourselves and others that Jesus is truly Lord of our lives. In those moments of sin, we make something else our lord instead of Jesus. When Peter realized what he had done, he didn't hide from the guilt that was rushing into his heart; he felt it fully: "Then Peter remembered the word of the Lord, how He had said to him, 'Before the rooster crows, you will deny Me three times.' So Peter went out and wept bitterly" (Luke 22:61–62 NKJV). Do we allow ourselves to feel the way Peter felt in that moment?

Peter's bitter tears were his confession, and at the news of the resurrection, he ran to Jesus! Peter didn't cower. He sprinted toward Jesus. After that, in those Easter days, he would have breakfast with Jesus on the beach, during which Jesus would restore Peter back to the right relationship with him. Not only that, Jesus commissioned Peter into a new season of joyful obedience, telling Peter to "Feed my sheep… [and] Follow Me" (John 21:17, 19). Guilt didn't ostracize Peter from Jesus. Through his guilt, by the power of Christ's death and resurrection, God restored Peter to new life and purpose.

THE CHURCH IN EPHESUS (REVELATION 2:4–5)

Western Christianity often forgets that repentance applies to entire congregations, not just individuals. Our individualistic culture has so shaped our worldview that it's challenging to consider things like corporate or systemic sin. If I'm describing you and your belief that sin only happens in an individual's heart, open your Bibles and read Revelation chapters 2 and 3. No single individual is called out in these chapters, only congregations.

The church in Ephesus was one such congregation. In Revelation 2, we hear Christ's message to them, "But I have this against you, that you have abandoned the love you had at first" (Revelation 2:4). Like many churches today, Ephesus had lost its first love. We may be going through the motions, but the love, the newness of life, and the joyful obedience are just gone. Here, Christ is calling this out for what it is: a sin against him! How do we know that's how Jesus views such malaise? Because he calls them to repent in the next verse, "Remember then from what you have fallen; repent..." (Revelation 2:5). We don't know the details of what happened next, but we know what they were warned would happen if repentance didn't occur, if they refused to step into and experience the guilt and repentance that Jesus clearly wanted them to experience. Jesus said, "If not, I will come to you and remove your lampstand from its place, unless you repent" (Revelation 2:5). Repentance would lead to new love, new zeal, and continued and growing light for the church in Ephesus. Unrepentance would mean the end to all of that. Should we expect any different if our congregations refuse to honestly self-examine and practice a life of continual and communal repentance before the Lord?

Salvation From Sorrow

Scripture reveals a God who calls both individuals and communities to deeper repentance. From Sinai to Isaiah, from Peter to Ephesus, good guilt is God's invitation to restoration. But this guilt is only the beginning. It awakens us to our need for repentance and renewal, yet through godly sorrow, repentance transforms into life-changing salvation.

Journal Prompt

- **Reflecting on God's Invitation Through Guilt:** Reflect on a time guilt stirred your heart—perhaps after a mistake or missed opportunity to honor God. Did you embrace that conviction like Peter, who wept and sought restoration, or did fear hold you back? Consider how accepting guilt as an invitation to repentance can renew your relationship with God. What step can you take this week to draw closer to Him?

CHAPTER 11 | GODLY SORROW—THE GATEWAY TO REPENTANCE

"Godly sorrow brings repentance that leads to salvation and leaves no regret, but worldly sorrow brings death" (2 Corinthians 7:10 NIV). That verse might turn heads, but by now, I hope it makes perfect sense. Neither Paul nor I claim guilt is enjoyable, but I'm not calling Christians to be masochists. What has become clear to me in scripture is that as unpleasant as a genuine sense of guilt can be, guilt that comes from the Holy Spirit in our lives is indeed a good thing. So good, in fact, it "leads to salvation."

There's no denying that the godly sorrow Paul refers to in 2 Corinthians is from God. He not only labels this sorrow that leads to salvation as "godly," but just before this verse, he says that the Corinthian church experienced such sorrow because of God Himself: "For you became sorrowful *as God intended...*" (2 Corinthians 7:9 NIV, emphasis added). Why does God use sorrow to lead us to salvation? Well, just as any precious metal needs to be purified by the dangerous and painful heat of the fire, godly sorrow—good guilt—is the refining fire that purifies us for God's purpose of both salvation into eternity, and salvation that begins here and now.

Godly Sorrow

As scripture affirms, godly sorrow—good guilt—comes from the Lord. The chain of events leading up to 2 Corinthians isn't as expressly transparent as we might like because while we have two letters from Paul to the Corinthian church, there are clues in both letters that there were at least two other letters to the Corinthians, totaling four letters in all between Paul and the Corinthians. And in the letter just before this one, Paul must have had one heck of a rebuke for the Corinthian church! After warnings, teachings, and instructions on living a holy and righteous life for Jesus, the Corinthian church still wasn't doing it. So, Paul essentially "let them have it" in the letter that is now lost to history, save its mention in 2 Corinthians. Good guilt isn't fun, nor should pastors enjoy calling for it; it's not about power or control. Paul exemplifies the true heart of a pastor when he describes what it felt like for him to write such a rebuke: "...I wrote you out of much distress and anguish of heart and with many tears..." (2 Corinthians 2:4). Again, the refining fire of godly sorrow isn't pleasant, but it is necessary, and it is good.

"Godly sorrow brings repentance that leads to salvation..." (2 Corinthians 7:10 NIV). This is the entire motivation behind Paul's heart, for it is the motivation of God's own heart. Paul didn't enjoy calling the Corinthians to the mat, and clearly, it wasn't a pleasant experience for the Corinthians either but look what came of it! I appreciate the way Pastor Eugene Peterson conveys Paul's pastoral heart when describing what Paul saw in the Corinthian's repentant hearts: "You're more alive, more concerned, more sensitive, more reverent, more human, more passionate, more responsible. Looked at from any angle, you've come out of this with purity of heart. And that is what I was hoping for in the first place..." (2 Corinthians 7:11–12 MSG). This is the very salvation Paul was aiming for. You see, salvation is not just something we experience when we die; it's an actual state of reverence, passion, humanity as God intended, and "purity of heart" that we can step into in our day-to-day lives right now. This is what good guilt, godly sorrow, leads to, and that's what God calls us to experience, not to turn away from.

Worldly Sorrow

But notice there's another type of sorrow that Paul lists in 2 Corinthians 7:10 (NIV): "worldly sorrow." This is the type of sorrow that a person has not for the fact that they sinned, but for the effects of that sin on their lives. It's selfish sorrow—distress not over sin but its consequences. Augustine of Hippo, a North African church leader from the 4th and 5th centuries, preached an Easter sermon on this passage from 2 Corinthians over 1,500 years ago and used a powerful illustration that both drives home the power of godly sorrow and the repulsiveness of worldly sorrow. To illustrate godly sorrow, Augustine likens it to the fertilizer (or "dung" as he originally said in his sermon) needed to produce a healthy crop of wheat: "...the wheat arrives at that luster, at that fine and beautiful appearance, by means of dung; the foulness was the path to a beautiful result." However, godly sorrow can easily be replaced by our selfish or worldly sorrow, as Paul stated. Instead of the dung being used in the field to produce a good crop, we could so easily throw the dung all over other places, other people, or even ourselves, not leaving us in a place of salvation at all but in a place of continued un-cleanness. As Augustine continued to preach: "...as I have said before, a suitable place for dung helps produce fruit but an unsuitable place leads to uncleanness."[1]

Judas Iscariot is a stark example of worldly sorrow: "When Judas, who had betrayed [Jesus], saw that Jesus was condemned, he was seized with remorse and returned the thirty pieces of silver to the chief priests and the elders. 'I have sinned,' he said, 'for I have betrayed innocent blood'" (Matthew 27:3–4 NIV). No one can look at Judas in this scene and say there was no sorrow. It's there as plain as day. But it was a sorrow he couldn't shake. There was no attempt to step closer to God in repentance. Instead, he tried to find absolution by returning the blood money he received from the religious leaders for turning Jesus in. It wasn't the act he was sorrowful about; it was how the act made him feel, and when nothing else could alleviate this worldly, selfish sorrow, it led only to destruction: "Then he went away and hanged himself" (Matthew 27:5 NIV). We can experience the sorrow that's from God, which leads to new life, or we can give into the sorrow of our own selfishness, which brings nothing but despair, misery, and loss. And yes, there is a way to ensure we're using this dung as fertilizer instead of just stepping deeper and deeper into it.

David's Sorrow in Psalm 51

Psalm 51 vividly portrays godly sorrow, leading to confession and restoration. Godly sorrow is more than just an emotional reaction; it's a transformative process. That distinction is key to navigating the difference between the godly sorrow that brings salvation and the worldly sorrow that brings death. If sorrow is only emotional, we'll either avoid it or be consumed by it. While clearly going through difficult emotions, David ultimately does not get lost in them. Instead, he gives himself to the Spirit and the God-given process of bringing his repentant heart before God to be restored to Him.

David begins Psalm 51 by fully admitting his sin: "Have mercy on me, O God... For I know my transgressions, and my sin is ever before me" (Psalm 51:1, 3). He's not only sorry for how his sin makes him feel; that would be selfish/worldly sorrow. He is sorry for the act of sinning itself. And do you remember the sin? This confession of David's is a heartfelt step

---

1. Gerald Bray and Thomas Oden, eds., *1–2 Corinthians*, ICCS/Accordance electronic ed, vol. 7, Ancient Christian Commentary on Scripture (Downers Grove, IL: InterVarsity Press, 1999), 267.

of repentance back to God after his act of adultery with Bathsheba and her husband Uriah's subsequent murder on the battlefield as an attempt to hide David's sin. These opening verses show the true humility in David's repentant heart. This is no superficial guilt but a profound realization, prompted by the Spirit, that he has violated God's holiness. Yet there is hope, for at least David is turning to God. It's as if David is aware that this conviction he's feeling isn't meant to condemn but to invite him to turn back to God.

The process continues in verse four when we read David's full-throated admission of guilt. He's not trying to hide anything. He's not trying to cast blame or obfuscate. He fully admits that he has "done what is evil in [God's] sight" and fully understands that any judgment or justice that comes his way is entirely justified. (Psalm 51:4). While worldly sorrow hides, godly sorrow, like David's good guilt here, includes a willingness to own up to our actions without excuse and acknowledge the depth of our wrongdoings before God.

Godly sorrow acknowledges our guilt but also trusts in God's forgiveness. David's prayer of confession reveals just such assurance in his heart of God's amazing grace: "Purge me with hyssop, and I shall be clean; wash me, and I shall be whiter than snow… Create in me a clean heart, O God, and put a new and a right spirit within me" (Psalm 51:7, 10). Godly sorrow brings us to our knees, grieving sin and seeking restoration.

Godly sorrow also includes a communal aspect as well. Earlier in this book, I shared that the most important ministry lesson I ever learned was that the very best thing I could offer to anyone, my wife, my children, my friends, and my church, was my personal walk of holiness. My experience of good guilt isn't just for my good; it's for yours, too! And your good guilt benefits me. David caught on to this in Psalm 51 as well, "then I will teach transgressors your ways, and sinners will return to you" (Psalm 51:13). Worldly sorrow has no such concern for others, only a selfish desire to protect one's pride, secure one's comfort, and reduce one's pain. There is no desire for the wellbeing of others when it comes to worldly sorrow. Godly sorrow, good guilt, realizes that to benefit others, to love others with the very love of God, means to repent and turn to God in one's own life.

Godly sorrow isn't the end; it's the start of renewal. By walking through conviction, acknowledgment, confession, and restoration, we experience the freedom and joy of being made whole in God's grace. This journey transforms us and equips us to share God's love. Godly sorrow refines us like a holy fire, burning away the impurities of sin and creating in us a clean heart and a right spirit. But the beauty of godly sorrow didn't stop in biblical times; it is a real path toward deeper intimacy with God and vibrant service in His kingdom today, becoming a source of lasting joy and spiritual growth for us and the communities around us.

Journal Prompt

- **Reflecting on Godly Sorrow in Your Life**: Recall a time of sorrow from a mistake. Did you respond with godly sorrow, leading to repentance, or worldly despair that leads to shame and destruction? Consider how turning to God, as in Psalm 51—acknowledging sin and trusting His grace—can turn guilt into freedom and joy. Write a prayer for a clean heart and guidance in His grace.

CHAPTER 12 | GODLY SORROW—THE GATEWAY TO HOPE

"Godly sorrow brings repentance that leads to salvation and leaves no regret" (2 Corinthians 7:10 NIV). In the last chapter, we explored how the Holy Spirit convicts us. Now, we'll focus on what follows: transformed lives. Guilt isn't the goal. God's purpose is restoration. Godly sorrow, different from worldly sorrow, doesn't lead to shame, fear, or hiding from God or our own wrongdoings. Godly sorrow leads to restoration.

And this isn't only a one-time thing. Just as the Corinthian church surely had more moments of godly sorrow, and just as the sin David confessed in Psalm 51 wasn't his only mistake, our experience of good guilt is the call of God on all our lives for the rest of our lives. Repentance isn't a one-time event or mere obligation. Repentance is a gracious invitation from God to continually turn more and more to Him throughout our lives, with the absolute guarantee from God, purchased by the blood of Christ on the cross. Through such repentance, we are assured we will flourish in God's grace. Repentance is not the finish line of salvation but the doorway to hope.

Holiness: The Journey and the Destination

My best trips were those where I enjoyed the journey as much as the destination. The destination is always the end goal; the journey would never occur without that destination in mind. Still, there's so much joy in the journey itself that the travel process becomes just as vital to the experience as anything else. I remember a recent Christmas trip to Disneyland with our then junior high and elementary age children. We woke up early on Christmas morning and had the kids open their gifts under the tree, all clues to a scavenger hunt. The clues eventually led them to the garage, where they saw their bags packed and ready to hit the road to California. We told them to go to the bathroom and brush their teeth, and we were on the road within five minutes! The day-long road trip was filled with Christmas music blasting on the car stereo, all of us grooving down the road in our Christmas jammies, and the kids enjoying their stockings filled with all the treats and car activities you could ever ask for. Our three incredible days at Disneyland were the highlight, but the journey was just as memorable. The goal was Disney, but we were abundantly blessed in the journey to get there!

Our destination as followers of Jesus is holiness. "You shall be holy, for I am holy," the Holy Spirit says through the words in 1 Peter 1:16. Our sin in the garden separated us from our original holy nature and the holy reality of God Himself. And from that moment, God's been yearning, working, and acting to get us back to that original state of perfect holiness so that He can have His children again in His presence. Holiness is the destination, and it is a joyful destination to pursue, as Dr. Steve Seamands of Asbury Seminary attests: "the life of holiness is not a life of gloom and doom. Holiness leads to happiness."[1] This happiness is not only found in the destination but on the journey before us, for the journey of holiness is just as important as the destination of holiness.

Recall our discussion of the means of grace in a previous chapter. These means are the common ways agreed upon by Christians and affirmed by scripture that God is regularly present and active in the lives of His people. Or, we could also say that the means of grace are how God continues to call us onto the journey of holiness so that we might arrive at our destination. One of those means or paths to holiness is our regular practice of repentance that flows from fully opening ourselves up to the Holy Spirit's conviction of good guilt in our lives.

We learned about Peter's experience of good guilt when he denied Jesus three times and the restoration he received from his honest pursuit of Jesus after the fact. He experienced true restoration from that grievous sin but wasn't finished on his journey to holiness. Peter didn't reach holiness all at once; he experienced the journey of holiness on his way there, which we can see with his continued life of following Jesus, as attested to the Book of Acts.

David's journey of following his God didn't end with Psalm 51. He still had many highs and lows ahead of him. There would be great moments of being faithful to God, but also moments of sin and the need to step into repentant living. I'm sure that what David learned in his experience of good guilt and repentance in Psalm 51 played out at other times throughout his life, each time longing for God to cleanse his sin and create a new heart within him. David's destination of holiness was reached after his journey of holiness.

---

1. Stephen Seamands, *Holiness of Heart and Life* (Wilmore, KY: Francis Asbury Press, 2022), 88.

The Joy of the Journey

I know guilt doesn't seem joyful. But biblical evidence shows that while guilt itself may not be a joyous emotion, the bridge that guilt takes us on leads to abundant joy. Joy isn't just for the future—God offers it now. And we can know it in many different ways.

We can experience the joy of walking through good guilt in our lives and our mental health. Positive Psychology shows that self-examination builds emotional agility, helping us process emotions instead of suppressing them. That sounds like a more joy-filled life to me.

Psychologists have also found that individuals who are humble enough to readily admit wrongdoings also see a reduction in anxiety and depression in their lives. The theory is that anxiety and depression are often the result of excessive self-centeredness in some people. When a regular practice of examining oneself takes place, that posture of self-centeredness becomes less prominent, which can then alleviate the debilitating symptoms of anxiety and depression. That sounds like a more joy-filled life to me.

In their studies, positive psychologists have also noticed mental and physical improvements in those willing to experience good guilt and repentance. Addressing guilt leads to improved physical health, including a noted reduction in coronary heart disease. That sounds like a more joy-filled life to me.

And remember, good guilt is good not only for the individual but also for those around them! PP has shown that regular repentance fosters humility, improving relationships through apologies and reparative actions. Also, each experience of good guilt fosters empathy, which can help us navigate toward peace and reconciliation in interpersonal conflicts. That sounds like a more joy-filled life to me.

And finally, we can't forget the already noted spiritual benefits of living through good guilt and the ensuing repentance it leads to. Regular repentance leads to a deeper intimacy with God, plain and simple. The more we experience His forgiveness, the more trust we'll have in the giver of that forgiveness to get us through anything, thick or thin. The more we openly share our faults with God, and even with other Christians, the more we take ourselves off the pedestal and place God there instead; the more our shame is reduced, and our confidence in our identity as new creations is increased. Hope is restored when we confess our sins. When we discover that good guilt is how we address our wrongdoings constructively, we realize we're not destroyed but lifted and brought into restored lives in God. And none of us ever know when our personal act of repentance may lead to a community revival that can last for weeks, months, or even years and decades. That sounds like a more joy-filled life to me!

And all of this is what God longs for us to experience *on the journey*! The destination hasn't even been reached yet, and we're already blessed with such amazing gifts from God! Christian positive psychologists King and Whitney rightly describe this journey as a blessing of God's grace: "In God's graciousness, he affords human creatures the time to become what they are supposed to be... God's Spirit works within the created realm to allow his creation to prosper and flourish...."[2] How blessed we are indeed to have God's destination of holiness in front of us and to know that as we journey there, we encounter and grow in holiness all along the way.

Embracing God's Invitation to Joy

God's invitation to good guilt is an invitation to joy. It's not an expectation that you live in gloom and doom, but a promise that happiness is yours as you step into the holiness that God calls you to. We can practice this daily. This is why I wake up every morning with one of the first prayers of my heart: "Lord Jesus Christ, Son of God, have mercy on me, for I have sinned." Praying that prayer in the morning forces me into a humble posture at the beginning of each day, which I know will only benefit me throughout the day.

What if you committed to begin your day with that prayer or something similar? Along with beginning your day in confession, consider ending it that way. The nightly process of self-examination is a Christian practice that goes back to our earliest church mothers and fathers. Regularly ask yourself and even journal through questions like, "Where have I failed to love today? Where have I resisted God's will?" I promise as you do this, you will grow less and less afraid to admit when you've been wrong and more and more ready to lay your guilt before the Lord because you'll grow in confidence in His willingness, desire, and ability to forgive all.

Consider how your church family practices confession together. If a corporate prayer of confession is prayed aloud on Sundays, do you balk at the idea? Do you even think much about it? Or are you just going through the motions like you've always done? If your pastor leads in prayer and asks for forgiveness on behalf the congregation, do you recognize your place in that prayer, or do you think to yourself, "My pastor must be talking about those other people?"

---

2. Pamela Ebstyne King and William B. Whitney, "What's the 'Positive' in Positive Psychology? Teleological Considerations Based on Creation and Imago Doctrines," *Journal of Psychology and Theology* 43, no. 1 (Spring 2015), 50.

Do you have a regular group of disciples you meet with, a small group of just 3–4 others who you know you can bring all your dirty laundry to because they won't chastise or judge you? Instead, they'll pray for you and pronounce forgiveness in the name of Jesus Christ over you. If you don't have that sort of group in your life, go to your pastor and ask them to help you find those people. If your pastor is the sort of pastor they should be, they will be blessed to walk with you in finding such brothers or sisters in the Lord to help you biblically experience good guilt.

We'll flesh out these practices and more later in the book, but let me end this chapter and end Part III with a simple call to embrace repentance as a source of hope and renewal in your life. You don't have to fear the experience of guilt, for it can be an altogether good thing for you and your church. As we wrap up this part and prepare to spend the next few chapters exploring how God has used good guilt in one of the largest movements of holiness in the past 300 years—the birth and spread of Methodism—let me leave you with this: What could God restore in your life if you stepped into repentance today? How might this invitation to renewal transform not only your heart but the lives of those around you? God can do that much and so much more.

Journal Prompt

- **Reflecting on Holiness:** Reflect on your journey with God. Where do you feel close to Him, and where is there distance? Ask the Holy Spirit to reveal where repentance could bring renewal. How might embracing godly sorrow lead to deeper intimacy and joy in your relationship with Him? Write a prayer of confession and a prompted action step week.

Part III Check-in

As we close Part III, take a moment to reflect on how shame, guilt, repentance, and godly sorrow are shaping your walk with God. Using the scale below, mark where you honestly find yourself:

-10 (Distant, burdened by shame) to +10 (Free, joyful in godly sorrow and repentance)

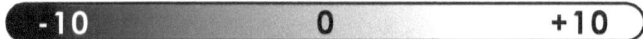

- Where do you land this week and why?

- Are you experiencing guilt that leads to repentance, or has shame been weighing you down? How can you lean into godly sorrow instead of worldly despair?

- If you feel stuck in shame, what step of faith might help you move forward? What truth do you need to hold onto about your identity in Christ?

- If you've moved into the positive, what has led to that renewal? How has embracing repentance deepened your sense of hope and joy?

Let this be a moment of honest reflection—God's grace meets us wherever we are, but He never leaves us there.

Part IV

THE DNA OF A MOVEMENT
(CHAPTERS 13–16)

CHAPTER 13 | FROM THE BEGINNING

None of what I've shared with you is new. Everything we've explored together is ancient stuff. However, what it has meant for me—and hopefully for you as well—has been a rediscovery of what God has desired for us all along. If you come from a Methodist/Wesleyan heritage like I do, you don't even have to look back very far in your religious tradition to find this. In fact, everything I've been advocating for in the first half of this book wasn't just part of how Methodism began; it was absolutely vital to its birth. Good guilt gave rise to the movement that I and countless others have been blessed to be part of for nearly 300 years.

A Life of Constant Confession from a Beginning of Constant Communion

Methodism's rise begins with John Wesley, the movement's founder. Born in 1703, Wesley was raised by Samuel, an Anglican priest, and Susanna, a devoted leader in her church. The constant call to repentance and confession would have been second nature to Wesley from a young age. Samuel Wesley, considered a radical sacramentalist, offered monthly communion at Epworth, unlike most priests, who served it only three times a year. Samuel's passion for frequent communion led him to write a curriculum for children. And in this curriculum, we see the strong connection between communion and the call to repent to God. He even wrote a prayer of repentance that the children could learn as they came to the Lord's Supper in their church:

> …Imprint, I beseech thee, in my mind, so lively a sense of my Saviour's sufferings, and let me receive, and carry away so lasting an impression of them from this sacrament [of communion], that I may henceforth die unto Sin, and live unto righteousness that I may subdue and mortifie more and more all criminal desires, and the whole body of death, thro' Jesus Christ my Lord. Amen![1]

---

1. Samuel Wesley, *The Pious Communicant Rightly Prepared, or, A Discourse Concerning the Blessed Sacrament* (London, England: Forgotten Books, 2018), 45.

I know it's a little different from the prayers we may teach our children today, but this was the reality for the children under Samuel's pastoring, and thus the reality for his son. Each time communion took place in that Epworth church, Wesley and everyone in the pews would consider how they needed to die more and more "unto sin" and "live more unto righteousness." That's repentance, plain and simple! That's the prodigal son's journey, turning away from a life of squandering our inheritance and returning to the newness of life in our Father's house.

Wesley began his life of faith grounded on a foundation of good guilt. He started following Jesus knowing that regular self-examination was not for shame or self-loathing but a practice that can lead to a new life in Christ, day by day. This is hinted at in his father's teaching on the benefits of such constant confession through regular communion: "The oftner the vows [of pardon] are renewed upon us… the more frequently we partake of this Bread of Life, the greater strength shall we receive in the inward man, and highest degrees of grace and assistance in God's service."[2] Samuel's call to come to Christ's table more often was a call to experience the conviction of the Holy Spirit's good guilt, and the power of God's forgiving grace through the life, death, and resurrection of the Son. It was a call that clearly impacted his son and one that Wesley would live into in ways beyond anyone's expectations.

From Doing to Being

The last thing I want is for any of us to think that a regular, ritualistic practice of praying a prayer of confession, journaling thoughts of self-examination, or even frequent communion is all it takes to experience the good guilt that leads to a new life. That would be legalism. And that's what Wesley's life quickly became once he entered adulthood and his career in ministry. He took all the lessons he learned from home and doubled down on the frequency of it all. Instead of praying just once a day, he would pray multiple times a day. Instead of just receiving communion once per month (as he learned from his father), he would receive it multiple times a week. Instead of occasionally visiting the poor and sick, he would do so as often as possible. You name the spiritual practice, he did it, and he did it to the max.

Wesley pursued confession to "do good" rather than to become holy. Like many today, Wesley believed religious acts would earn him favor with God. One historian described Wesley's approach to following Jesus with words like

2. Wesley, *The Pious Communicant Rightly Prepared, or, A Discourse Concerning the Blessed Sacrament*, 67.

"scrupulous regularity" and "meticulous... slavish obedience" to arbitrary laws.[3] Wesley's rigid repentance was not God's desire for him or us.

Wesley's rigid and legalistic practices certainly didn't bring him joy and newness of life. In fact, after years of living with such scrupulous religiosity, he found himself in a place of deep spiritual darkness. He often questioned his role as a religious leader in the Church of England and even questioned his own salvation. Guilt for guilt's sake didn't bring Wesley any hope or promise; it brought only shame—the constant reminder that he alone could never live up to God's great expectations for what human flourishing could be like. Imagine year after year of doing anything and everything to please God, moment after moment of groveling before the Almighty, with zero assurance that any of it did any good whatsoever. That was John Wesley's reality as he was entering his mid-30s. No good seemed to come of his practices, only self-condemnation that he could never live up to the righteous living he believed was necessary to truly know God's love.

All of this would change on the evening of May 24, 1738. That night, Wesley was invited to attend the Moravian prayer meeting on Aldersgate Street in London that we discussed in a previous chapter. Barely minutes into the gathering, God did what God does best and moved mightily in Wesley's heart to bring true conviction of sin and full assurance of pardon through Jesus Christ. Later, writing of that moment, Wesley professed, "I did trust in Christ, Christ alone for salvation: and an assurance was given me, that he had taken away my sins, even mine, and saved me from the law of sin and death."[4] At that moment, God assured Wesley that there was nothing he did or could ever do to earn more of God's love in his life; it was everything that God had already done through Jesus Christ that showed Wesley all the love he could ever know and then some! At that moment, Wesley's approach to spiritual practices, including repentant living, shifted from doing them in hope that they'd save him, to trusting that he was already *being* saved. Thus, he could do them with complete confidence that God was already at work in his life through them.

Wesley was living out what the scripture teaches us still today in 1 John. Wesley was no longer afraid to face the realities of his own sin but instead trusted God to fully pardon and forgive, for "if anybody does sin, we have an advocate with the Father—Jesus Christ, the Righteous One. He is the atoning sacrifice for our sins..." (1 John 2:1–2 NIV). Wesley would not approach

---

3. Irwin Reist, "John Wesley's View of the Sacraments: A Study in the Historical Development of a Doctrine," *Wesleyan Theological Journal 6*, no. Spring (1971): 43.

4. John Wesley, *The Works of John Wesley: Journal from October 14, 7735, to November 29, 1745*, Third Edition, vol. 1 (Grand Rapids, MI: Baker Books, 1996), 103.

guilt as something he had to work his way out of by his own actions, but now as the "godly grief… that leads to salvation…" (2 Corinthians 7:10).

Repentance was no longer a desperate plea for favor but a confident step into God's assurance. Now, after his Aldersgate experience, he would view, practice, and teach repentant living differently. He was no longer a person *doing* repentant things to be saved; he was now *being* a saved person in Christ who was free to live the repentant life God had always called him to live, not in shame of never living up but in confidence of God's ability to work mighty things through whatever good guilt the Holy Spirit would convict his heart with. He went from being a hard-liner on seemingly every spiritual practice you can think of to living with an actual "heart religion that would define [his]… outlook and evangelical impulses throughout the rest of his life."[5] And, he would preach the importance of regular repentance for the rest of his life as well.

Journal Prompt

- **Reflecting on Your Spiritual Practices**: Consider your approach to repentance and spirituality. Are you focused more on "doing" right or "being" in God's grace? Reflect on ways to shift from striving to resting in His forgiveness like John Wesley after Aldersgate. How might this change bring freedom and joy to your relationship with God?

---

5. Ryan Nicholas Danker, *Wesley and the Anglicans* (Downers Grove, IL: InterVarsity Press, 2016), 57.

CHAPTER 14 | "RISE YE WORMS…"

Pardon, and power, and peace,
And perfect righteousness
From that sacred Fountain springs;
Wash'd in His all-cleansing blood
Rise, ye worms, to priests and kings,
Rise in Christ and reign with God.[1]

Try finding a modern worship song that calls Christians "worms" like Charles Wesley did. We are people who are wholly uncomfortable with the idea of putting ourselves down too much. We accept light self-deprecation, but much worship music often prioritizes comfort over reverence. I'm generalizing, of course. Some deep worship songs exist today, but I fear they're often the exceptions to the norm. And this isn't just regarding the songs we sing, but our entire Western approach to Christian discipleship. However, there was a day and time, especially in the Methodist world, when the verse I quoted above wasn't the exception; it was the norm.

The logic of common American evangelical culture might lead us to think that after John Wesley's Aldersgate experience, he did not need to worry himself with things like repentance, confession, guilt, and sin anymore. He had finally "become a Christian" by believing in Jesus' blood on the cross for the forgiveness of his sins. And that's sufficient, right? That would only be partly true. After Aldersgate, Wesley no longer had to prove himself before God, yet his repentance deepened. He no longer needed to prove himself before God, for he lived with the assurance of Christ in his life. But this assurance didn't decrease his acts of repentant living or his willingness to step into good guilt. No, the opposite took place. He wanted to live even deeper into repentance because he had more assurance of Christ in his life than ever before. Repentance was no longer a way to "get saved" but a means of grace to

---

1. John Wesley and Charles Wesley, "Hymns on the Lord's Supper," in *The Eucharistic Hymns of John and Charles Wesley*, by J. Ernest Rattenbury (Eugene, OR: Wipf and Stock Publishers, 2014), 207.

deepen salvation. In Christ, he was indeed a new creation, but a new creation with the constant conviction in his heart of good guilt reminding him that as a "worm" he was constantly called to rise and "reign with God."

God's House of Salvation

A metaphor that has helped Methodists understand God's gift of salvation is that of a warm, protective, comforting house. Wesley himself used this metaphor in a sermon titled "The Scripture Way of Salvation." In this sermon, he saw the journey of salvation as three phases of God's grace in our lives.

First, there is prevenient grace. We experience this grace from God while approaching and standing upon the front porch of God's house. This is the grace that "precedes" from God to us even before we know God's gracious work in our lives. This is the grace that we believe is living and active in all people's hearts, minds, and souls. We believe nothing happens apart from God's grace. This grace sustains life and stirs awareness of right and wrong before we know Jesus. Anything good and true that is living and active in the life of a non-believer is not by their own power but by the power of God in their life through prevenient grace. This grace brings a person to that initial point of wondering if they just might not live up to the ideal version of themselves. It's this grace that plants those initial seeds of good guilt in a person's life and calls them to consider that they may need to turn to something, somebody, greater than themselves for forgiveness and pardon that brings newness of life, hope, and joy.

Prevenient grace leads to justifying grace—stepping over the threshold into God's saving love. It is the moment of that first confession of sin before God and the experience of forgiveness by the blood of Christ on the cross. Justifying grace takes place in that instant, confessing that Jesus is Lord and believing that God raised him from the dead.

Many in Western Christianity stop their journey here. In 2011, the Barna Group released the results of a 10-year, 15,000-participant study that tracked the status of Christian faith across the American population.[2] The study tracked people's views on sin, forgiveness, and transformation. Here are the results from that study:

Percentage of Americans	Religious Stage
1%	Unaware of Sin
16%	Indifferent to Sin
39%	Worried about Sin

2. George Barna, *Maximum Faith: Live Like Jesus*, 2011.

9%	Forgiven from Sin
24%	Forgiven and Active in the Church
6%	Holy Discontent
3%	Broken by God
1%	Surrender and Submission
0.5%	Profound Love for God
0.5%	Profound Love for People

JD Walt, Methodist pastor and stalwart advocate for a wholesale reinvigoration of discipleship within Methodism, sees clear evidence in these numbers that the American church has, by and large, only been concerned with getting people "in the door." Walt summarizes our ministry approach like this: "You're a sinner. You need a savior. Pray this prayer and you're forgiven. Now get involved in the church."[3] But our Christian journey doesn't begin and end with justifying grace. There's more of God's grace to experience, and, as we see with those graces laid on top of the same data, there's much work to be done to get people to keep walking deeper into God's house.

Percentage of Americans	Religious Stage		
1%	Unaware of Sin	Prevenient & Justifying Grace	89% either on the porch or just inside God's house
16%	Indifferent to Sin		
39%	Worried about Sin		
9%	Forgiven from Sin		
24%	Forgiven and Active in the Church		
6%	Holy Discontent	Sanctifying Grace	11% actively walking deeper into God's house of grace.
3%	Broken by God		
1%	Surrender and Submission		
0.5%	Profound Love for God		
0.5%	Profound Love for People		

3. JD Walt, "The Journey to Awakening: Embracing the Second Half of the Gospel," YouTube, (The Woodlands, TX: The Woodlands Methodist Church, 2023), 9:02 to 9:10, https://www.youtube.com/watch?v=tltrCSnPWNo.

God's sanctifying grace calls us deeper into His love, beyond the doorway of salvation. Yet, according to the data above, only 11% of the U.S. population is actively pursuing such a deep connection with God's love (and I bet that number is even less now, over a decade after this study was released). I'm especially intrigued by the language Barna used to describe several stages in the "Sanctifying Grace" half of this journey: *Holy Discontent, Broken by God, Surrender and Submission*. This isn't the language of people who are "good to go" with their faith. No, this is the language of people who would resonate with that early Methodist hymn verse to "rise ye worms." This is the language and posture of people open to the prospect of good guilt in their lives, not for self-loathing but for increased hope and confidence in the newness of life and joyful obedience that comes with moving more into God's house!

What Barna reveals as lacking in America, Wesley built into Methodism 300 years ago. Wesley didn't just have his Aldersgate conversion and think, "I'm good to go." No, he had his experience and then spent the rest of his life moving deeper into God's house and getting as many people as possible to move there with him. As I've already said elsewhere, our call as Methodists is not only to get people into heaven, but to get heaven into us as much as possible here, now, today! Wesley said likewise about the mission of the Methodist church when he said that the preaching, promoting, and calling people to God's sanctifying grace, calling them deeper into God's house, is "the grand depositum which God has lodged with the people called Methodists; and for the sake of propagating this chiefly He appeared to have raised us up."[4]

And how did Wesley do this? Well, plenty of converts were made throughout Wesley's life. Plenty of people were brought through the door of Justification. But they weren't left at the door; they were invited deeper through repentance. They met weekly in small groups, asking questions like: "How is it with your soul?" and "What sins do you need to confess?" Through these questions, Methodists were regularly confronted with the Spirit's good guilt in their life, and they couldn't hide from the necessary practice of honest self-examination that comes with venturing deeper into God's house.

Early Methodists practiced "constant communion," receiving it as often as possible. And, for the 18th-century Anglican, this meant that every time you received holy communion, you had the experience of corporately and publicly confessing your sins together before God—the two went hand in hand according to the Anglican Book of Common Prayer (the book teaching how Christian worship, including holy communion, was practiced in

---

4. John Wesley, "Letter to Robert C. Brackenbury, Esq.," in *The Works of John Wesley*, vol. 13 (Grand Rapids, MI: Baker Books, 1996), 9.

England). As Early Methodists constantly communed, they also constantly confessed as they constantly explored God's house together.

Early Methodists were required to regularly interact with and minister to the sick, poor, and outcasts—experiences that have the effect of bringing good guilt to a person's soul, good guilt in the form of conviction of selfish pursuits and a lack of initiative to do more to pursue justice for the down and out. These practices of visiting the sick and poor, constantly receiving holy communion, and actively participating in small discipleship groups all helped build up a movement that became so much more than just getting people through the stages of prevenient and justifying grace, but a movement that yearned to get people into God's house of grace. And it didn't happen by turning away from feelings of guilt, but by leaning into people's "holy discontent," by acknowledging their "brokenness before God," and calling people to a place of "surrender and submission." It happened by inviting people into an honest experience with good guilt, so that, even though we're but worms, we hear God's call to "Rise ye worms" and to "reign with Christ" as we live more fully in God's house than ever before.

Journal Prompt

- **Experiencing Good Guilt in the House of Grace:** Reflect on your place in the "house of salvation." Are you on the porch, just inside the door, or moving into God's grace? How does the Holy Spirit provoke "holy discontent" in your heart, urging growth? Identify one step you can take this week—confession, accountability, or service—to respond to this conviction and draw closer to God's transformative love.

CHAPTER 15 | SWEET REPENTANCE

The good guilt embraced by John Wesley sparked a revival that still ripples today. Holiness denominations like the Church of the Nazarene and the Wesleyan Church trace their roots to this movement. Even Pentecostalism, shaped by Wesleyan theology, emerged from a longing for deeper holiness, as seen in the Azusa Street Revival. If you are part of a church that practices small groups in any form, you have John Wesley's early Methodists to thank, as they were adamant that being faithful to God meant connecting with other Christians and being willing to be vulnerable, honest, and yes, even confess sins to one another.

All this to say… much that began with and continued from the birth of Methodism has had to do with an evangelistic zeal to reach new people for Christ, but what had to come *first* within their hearts before they could preach that others turn from sin was that they would turn from sin more and more in their own lives. Repentance isn't just for non-believers—God calls His people to continually turn from sin. For if we are a people who claim salvation, then the continually repentant lives of Christians are "nothing less than the very substance of salvation."[1]

Remembering our Telos

Positive Psychology's goal of flourishing aligns closely with the Christian pursuit of holiness. It uses the language of "flourishing" to refer to its telos (a fancy term with Greek roots meaning "end goal"). And is that not the telos for those of us in Christ as well? We yearn to flourish as new creations today and hope for our ultimate flourishing when Jesus returns. Too often, we focus on future flourishing and neglect the transformation God offers now. So, what's really the underlying thinking here? What was it about how early Methodists lived that led to such vibrant spiritual flourishing in their lives in

1. Kenneth J. Collins, *The Scripture Way of Salvation: The Heart of John Wesley's Theology* (Nashville, TN: Abingdon Press, 1997), 29.

England 300 years ago—a flourishing so profound that many are still experiencing its reverberations today?

The Christian Life of Repentance

Wesley distinguished between "legal" repentance (initial conviction of sin) and "evangelical" repentance (ongoing transformation). Because the word "evangelical" has become so bogged down not only by the commercialization of late 20th and early 21st century Christian culture (but also by American politics), it's important that we ask what Wesley meant by labeling these two repentances this way.

When Wesley spoke of "legal" repentance, he specifically referred to the repentance that first leads to a relationship with Jesus as Lord. To return to our house analogy, this is the repentance that occurs when someone steps through the door of the house (justifying grace). This represents that "thorough conviction of sin" that God works in a person's life to draw them through the door and into forgiveness through Christ on the cross (see John Wesley's personal notes on Matthew 3:8). However, remember that this is not the end of repentant living. Wesley continues to discuss "evangelical" repentance, which he defined as "a change of heart (and consequently of life) from all sin to all holiness."

Evangelical repentance deepens our relationship with Christ beyond the initial step of faith. Faith isn't just entering the house, it's exploring every room, growing in holiness. It's a lifelong attitude of openness to God's transformative work, permitting His grace to mold us day by day. This type of repentance doesn't just avoid sin; it actively propels us toward a life of greater holiness. For Wesley and his followers, this continual turning from sin was not optional but a central tenet of their faith. It was this sustained posture of repentance that empowered the early Methodists to experience remarkable spiritual vitality and flourishing, creating a foundation for revival that transformed lives and communities. As Christians today, embracing this same regularity of repentance helps us align more fully with God's purposes, contributing not only to our individual growth but also to the collective renewal of our congregations and beyond.

The "Sweetness" of Repentance

Like you and me, Wesley had some favorite devotional authors, from ancient church fathers like Augustine and Chrysostom to mystic thinkers like

Thomas A. Kempis and Teresa of Avila and reformers like Martin Luther and John Calvin. One of his favorites, Francis de Sales, a Catholic spiritual guide who lived and died about 100 years before Wesley, profoundly impacted Wesley's approach to the need for Christians to repent and the fruit that God can produce from such continual repentance.

Wesley cherished Francis de Sales' *An Introduction to the Devout Life*, requiring it for Methodist preachers to read. Why this book? In it, Wesley believed Francis to have written "strongly and scripturally on sanctification."[2] Sanctification is that journey of walking deeper and deeper into God's house of salvation. What, if anything, does Francis have to say in support of this notion that repentance is not just to become a Christian but to stay a Christian? Does Francis agree that such repentant living doesn't leave one in gloom and doom but instead leads to happiness? Absolutely!

Repentance is needed not just to become a Christian but to stay a Christian

First, Francis paints a vivid illustration that sin still plays a role in the Christian's life, and thus Christians still have the need to repent:

> A soul which having forsaken actual sin is yet always encumbered with this languishing inclination, reminds me of a person who is not ill, and yet is pale, ailing in all his functions--eating without appetite, sleeping without rest, laughing without gladness, and who instead of walking briskly, drags himself wearily along. Such a soul performs good actions, but with such spiritual languor as to deprive them of all grace, and to make them scanty and ineffective.[3]

You can follow Jesus, but unaddressed sin hinders true flourishing. Many of us follow Jesus like pale, weary stragglers. Or, to go back to PP, this sounds a lot like the individuals who go from negative 10 to zero (or positive one on a good day) in their walk of faith. However, Francis, Wesley, and early Methodists believed such a "scanty and ineffective" life does not have to be the norm for the Christian believer. We don't have to settle for zero or positive one; we can experience positive ten!

---

2. John Wesley, *Selections from the Writings of the Rev. John Wesley*, ed. Herbert Welch (New York, NY: Eaton & Mains, 1901), 85.

3. Francis de Sales, *Philothea, or An Introduction to the Devout Life* (Gastonia, NC: Tan Classics, 2009), 19.

God's call of repentance is on each disciple's heart. It's not a repentant life of misery that we're called to or one of bemoaning our brokenness, but rather a life where true "sweetness" can be found, even sweetness from guilt:

> If we are truly humble… we shall grieve bitterly over our sin because it offends God, but *we shall find sweetness in accusing ourselves*, because in doing so we honor Him; and *we shall find relief in fully revealing our complaints to our physician*… Hesitate not then to open your heart fully in Confession for in proportion as your sins go forth, the precious merits of Christ's Passion will come in and fill you with all blessings.[4]

As Francis de Sales and Wesley taught, continual repentance reveals the good guilt that leads to renewal and joy. In confession, as sin is cast out, Christ's redeeming love flows in, filling us with grace and blessing. This "sweetness" of repentance transforms us, leading to a flourishing life in God's grace.

Flourishing Together

Repentance isn't just personal; it's a collective pursuit. Early Methodists sought holiness together. When we gather in confession, we address our collective heart and recognize how sin impacts us as a community. In doing so we open ourselves to God's grace in a way that fortifies the entire church. Communal repentance encourages the Spirit to work within us as individuals and through us as a body, making us more faithful witnesses to the world.

Wesley emphasized corporate confession—through communion, song, and small groups. These moments helped the church reflect, repent, and realign with God's purposes. When the church confesses together, it creates space for God to bring healing and renewal that can last for centuries. I am part of God's fruit birthed out of the repentant living of John Wesley and early Methodists, and perhaps you are too. It's in these moments of communally repentant living that we remember we're not just individual Christians—we're part of something much bigger, and we flourish best when we step into good guilt together so that we can move toward holiness as one body.

The life of repentance isn't something we do alone, nor is it meant to end with us. When we embrace both personal and communal repentance, we cultivate a church alive with God's grace, a community moving toward holi-

---

4. Francis de Sales, *Philothea, or An Introduction to the Devout Life*, 47–48. Emphasis added.

ness and bringing the hope of restoration to the world around us. This is the flourishing life that God invites us into—together.

Journal Prompt

- **The Sweetness of Repentance in My Life**: Reflect on a moment when you felt the "sweetness" of repentance, either through personal confession or within a community. How did recognizing your sin lead to renewal, healing, or joy? Consider how embracing guilt regularly can enhance your spiritual growth and strengthen your connections with God and others. Write about one practical step you can take this week to practice repentance personally or communally.

CHAPTER 16 | WE'VE FORGOTTEN HOW TO BE REPENTANT PEOPLE

The renewal of the church depends on reclaiming continual repentance—not guilt for guilt's sake, but "good guilt" that leads to joy and transformation. So, what happened? If repentance was central to Methodism, where did we go wrong?

Much ink has been put to paper to figure all of this out and much has been discovered. Leading authors and teachers in recent years have helped us realize the great harm that occurred to the Methodist church in the U.S. when the accountable small groups, Class and Band meetings, were abandoned in the mid-1800s. I hope by now it makes sense what a grave mistake this was on our walk of faith together as Methodists. Without these regular occasions for men and women of faith to gather weekly and *confess* good guilt to one another, it is easy for us to neglect such confession altogether. I hope to add another argument to why we've forgotten how to be people who practice good guilt together. We've neglected it not only in our small groups' lives but in our lives of corporate worship as well.

Constant Confession: A Refresher

Methodists once practiced constant confession and communion. The revival in England was both evangelical and sacramental, restoring baptism and communion as true means of grace. Holy Communion for early Methodists wasn't just supposed to be regular but *constant*. By the end of his life, Wesley received communion four times a week—not out of legalism, but a desire to walk closer with God. In Wesley's day, communion always included public confession and God's assurance of pardon. Constant communion did not happen without constant confession, and constant confession did not happen without constant communion. They were part and parcel of the same means of grace.

The early Methodists' singing was key to the experience of good guilt together in Holy Communion. Of the 166 communion hymns that Charles Wesley (John Wesley's brother) wrote for early Methodists to sing during the communion service, it is hard to find one that does not have the singer humbly declare through song their need for God's forgiveness in their lives (Remember "Rise ye worms" from chapter 14?). Here is a sampling of three verses out of 166 hymns. These verses were sung by believing Christians, already assured of their salvation in Christ, yet they still sang of their deep need for Christ's forgiveness in their lives because of their sin. Notice in each how sin is still very publicly confessed and done so with the hope and promise of God's forgiveness through Christ's sacrificed and risen body:

By thine agonizing pain
And bloody sweat, we pray,
By thy dying love to man,
Take all our sins away:
Burst our bonds, and set us free;
From all iniquity release;
O Remember Calvary,
And bid us go in peace![1]

Let Thy blood, by faith applied,
The sinner's pardon seal;
Speak us freely justified,
And all our sickness heal;
By Thy passion on the tree
Let all our griefs and troubles cease.[2]

Father, behold Thy dying Son!
Even now He lays our ransom down,
Even now declares our sins forgiven;
His flesh is rent, the living way
Is open'd to eternal day,
And lo, through Him we pass to heaven![3]

At Methodism's healthiest, an order of worship was embraced and regularly used that often included corporate prayers of confession and pardon and

---

1. Wesley and Wesley, "Hymns on the Lord's Supper," 200.

2. Wesley and Wesley, *The Eucharistic Hymns of John and Charles Wesley*, 41.

3. Wesley and Wesley, *The Eucharistic Hymns of John and Charles Wesley*, 70.

the singing of these 166 communion hymns as part of the corporate body of Christ receiving Holy Communion together. This repentant practice, this collective self-examination and willingness to go through good guilt together, along with the vibrant accountable discipleship groups, Bands (3–5 people, same gender) and Classes (10–15, coed), is how God brought revival and kept revival going. So much so that the revival "crossed the pond" and planted itself here in the U.S. However, I believe that decisions made in the beginning years of American Methodism damaged our understanding of good guilt so much that we're still reeling from it to this day.

The Vanishing of Constant Confession

To understand this shift, we must ask: What did Wesley want for American Methodism? We see his intent in *The Sunday Service*, Wesley's published worship guide for American Methodists. His own words speak to the purpose behind *The Sunday Service* when he wrote that he had "furnished [the American Methodist church with] forms of worship… in a slightly revised and abridged Prayer Book called *The Sunday Service*."[4] And this very book, which Wesley himself published, included the same corporate prayers of confession and the same assurance of God's forgiveness that Wesley and every Methodist in England would have been so familiar with and used each time they received communion together. Wesley hoped American Methodists would continue the practices of constant communion and confession, but they were abandoned before they were even tried. A few years after Wesley gave American Methodists *The Sunday Service*, it was "laid aside and… never used since in public worship."[5]

American Methodists not only ignored Wesley's resources but officially abandoned practices of corporate confession early on. By 1792, in the first document outlining American Methodism's doctrines and disciplines, the church had officially moved away from Early Methodism's practice of constant communion (and thus constant confession). Wesley's desire for American Methodists was for them to receive communion "on every Lord's Day," that is, every Sunday.[6] How can God's people constantly confess together

---

4. John Wesley, "To 'Our Bretheren in America,'" in *John Wesley*, ed. Albert C. Outler (New York, NY: Oxford University Press, 1964), 361.

5. Jesse Lee, *A Short History of the Methodists in the United States of America Beginning in 1766, and Continued till 1809* (Baltimore, MD: Magill and Clime Booksellers, 1810), 107, http://archive.org/details/shorthistoryofme00leej.

6. Wesley, "To 'Our Bretheren in America,'" 84.

and experience one of the fullest expressions of God's hope and promise of forgiveness if they do not constantly commune together?

American Methodists not only abandoned constant communion, but officially, they weakened the connection that good guilt/repentance/confession plays in the Lord's Supper. In that same 1792 book of church law where the expectation of constant communion was eliminated, they also allowed Methodist pastors and congregations to "omit any part of the [communion] service, except for the prayer of Consecration."[7]

The 166 communion hymns, essential to the Methodist practice and understanding of repentance and assurance, were never widely used in America. They were never published in a single volume in America, even though they had been published numerous times in England. (Sad fact: they've still *never* been published for church use in the U.S.). By 1872, only 23 of Wesley's 166 communion hymns remained in the U.S. Methodist hymnal. Today, only four remain in *The United Methodist Hymnal* (1989). One of the most profound ways that early Methodists experienced good guilt together was by singing about it around the communion table. This practice never took hold in American Methodism.

While I'm thankful for efforts by ministries like *Seedbed* for publishing new Methodist hymnals, such as *Our Great Redeemers Praise*, and the increasing number of the 166 communion hymns within these new hymnals, I long for the day when all 166 are available to congregations across our nation and that they're sung humbly in the way we collectively confess our sins through them, and they're sung boldly in the way we profess our assurance that God can and will work through our collective good guilt to forgive our sins through the blood of the cross and the broken body of Jesus Christ.

Time for a Reclamation!

There's no doubt in my heart, mind, or soul that early Methodism thrived in large part because God's people experienced good guilt through Holy Communion. Through such repentant hearts, early Methodists experienced God's promise of new life and a hope that they could obey His call to holiness, not out of fear, duty, or obligation but out of joyful obedience and newness of life. Vital aspects of these means of grace, though abandoned here

---

7. *The Doctrines and Discipline of the Methodist Episcopal Church in America*, (1792), 233, https://divinityarchive.com/handle/11258/16726.

in the U.S., can be recaptured and reclaimed once again! We may have forgotten repentance, but all is not lost. We can reclaim it as central to our faith.

Journal Prompt

- **Reflecting on the Past**: Consider how infrequent confession and repentance affect your spiritual journey and church life. How can you reclaim practices like communal confession, frequent communion, or confession-focused songs? Describe one step you or your church can take to reintroduce repentance in worship and encourage renewal.

Part IV Check-In

As we conclude Part IV, take time to reflect on how the themes of these chapters—Wesley's legacy of repentance, the power of communal confession, and the loss (and potential recovery) of these practices—are shaping your walk with God.

Using the scale below, mark where you honestly find yourself: -10 (Distant, burdened by guilt) to +10 (Free, joyful in repentance)

- Where do you land this week and why?

- Do you resonate with Wesley's renewed joy in repentance after Aldersgate, or do you struggle with repentance as duty rather than grace?

- Has your church's approach to confession and repentance shaped your spiritual life? Are there aspects of early Methodism's practices that you long to reclaim?

- If you feel distant or hesitant, what's keeping you from stepping further into God's house of grace? What spiritual practice—personal or communal—might help you move forward?

- If you've found renewed joy through repentance, how can you continue deepening that experience and encouraging others to do the same?

Take this as a moment for honest reflection. Repentance is not a burden—it's the invitation into deeper intimacy with God. His grace meets us where we are, but it never leaves us there.

Part V

MAKE REPENTANCE COOL AGAIN (CHAPTERS 17–20)

CHAPTER 17 | REPENTANCE HAS A PR PROBLEM

"…we are ambassadors for Christ…" (2 Corinthians 5:20).

Let that sink in.

We are ambassadors for Christ.

We are ambassadors for Christ!

Repentance isn't just for non-believers—it's God's call for all of us, always. Yet, too often, it's viewed as shame-ridden and uncomfortable rather than life-giving. As Western Christians, we exist in a society that has a ferocious appetite for comfort, and this comfort has led to cultural avoidance. This cycle of avoidance, Positive Psychologists observe, continually makes us more and more psychologically immune "to circumstances that are less comfortable and more inconvenient."[1] In other words, the more we avoid the discomfort of guilt, the harder and harder it gets to trust that it can truly be part of God's good will for our lives.

Repentance has a PR problem—God calls it a gift, but the world sees it as shame. The best way to change that? The church must embody it well. Because remember, *we are ambassadors for Christ!* We are not called to represent a world that makes comfort-seeking and avoiding responsibility our societal foundation. We are called to represent our Lord, who beckons us to fully own up to our mistakes, failures, and sins because Christ himself exists "to be the offering for our sin, so that we could be made right with God through Christ" (2 Corinthians 5:21 NLT). And as Paul continues in 2 Corinthians 6:1, "…we beg you not to accept this marvelous gift of God's kindness and then ignore it" (NLT). *We are ambassadors for Christ.* We have been promised that by the power of Christ on the cross, we can humbly repent of our sins before the Lord and be reconciled to him to be his ambassadors. Let's not just live as if we've only accepted this gift the one time when we first became a Christian, but let's embrace it always, and in doing so, let's be the very best PR agents for the hope of repentance that Christ offers to the world.

---

1. Kashdan and Biswas-Diener, *The Upside of Your Dark Side*, 27–28.

It Starts With Us

Right now, we can be Christ's ambassadors. Our own hearts and congregations need revival. I promise that in every congregation there's been a desire to brush past mistakes and ignore sinful ministry decisions (and indecisions). Even if you can't think of any specifics (which I find unlikely), still speak these words with me. Yes, *speak* them, even if it's just a whisper under your breath while reading this at your local coffee shop. There's great power in the spoken word. God created this universe with spoken words. Spoken words in Christ have power, not because they're magic but because they too, when spoken in Spirit and in truth, are means of grace by which God does mighty things. So, humble yourself. Trust everything you've learned so far. Don't brush aside guilt. Don't hide from mistakes. Don't give in to the shame that Satan wants you to feel. Trust in God's promise of hope. Don't ignore God's great gift of reconciliation and forgiveness offered in Christ. Embrace it, as you say with me, as you repent with me—repenting of our unrepentant hearts. Ok, here we go:

> *Lord Jesus Christ, Son of God, have mercy and forgive us. We have been an unrepentant people. Amen.*

Now, hear the Good News of the Gospel: *Christ died for us while we were yet sinners, and that proves God's love for us. In the name of Jesus Christ, you are forgiven!* And in that moment, you did one of the most powerful things you could ever do for your Christian witness to the world; you didn't take Christ's Good News for granted. You didn't just stand at the doorway of God's house. On a scale from -10 to +10, you didn't settle for 0. You didn't succumb to gloom and doom. You embraced good guilt, and I believe God will only work hope, newness of life, and joyful obedience because of it.

Facing Hard Truths Together

After pastoring three churches, I know how rare that moment was. We don't like to talk about sin (unless it's the sin of "those people out there"). And to be honest, it's not fun for us pastors to talk about your sin, either. Preaching on topics we know will tickle your ears and bring warm fuzzies to your hearts is way more fun. It is ever apparent to me that the culture around repentance within our congregations is not a Gospel-shaped culture, but a culture shaped by the world around us. We've been "evangelized" by the world to avoid admitting our wrongdoings at all costs.

When I ask churches why younger generations are leaving, the response is usually blame—on the youth, their parents, or culture—rather than self-examination. "The world has changed too much." "No one wants to go to church anymore." "Parents don't make church a priority anymore." I could go on and on about how it has become far too easy for us to blame things outside of ourselves. And you know what? I agree with each of those statements. Fewer people want to go to church. The world has changed dramatically. And parents don't make church a priority for their families anymore. Those things can all be true, and I believe they are valid. However, that doesn't mean that our congregations haven't made ministry decisions, and possibly sinful ones at that, which have also contributed to the decline of younger generations in our churches.

For many American Christians, confession is foreign. As we have seen, over a third of self-identified Christians report never having confessed their sins to God.[2] One-third of Christians! That's over 30% of people who claim to follow Jesus and also say that they haven't even done that initial act of confession of sin to step into God's house. They think they're in the house, but they're still just on the porch.

Our culture has conditioned us to avoid admitting wrongs. We have an American culture that does not practice scriptural Christianity when it comes to repentant living. And that's what makes our prayer of confession at the beginning of this chapter so radical and necessary. Repentance has a PR problem not just in our world but within the walls of our churches. It's time for you and me to stand up (or, rather, to fall on our knees) and exemplify such repentant living to our own brothers and sisters in Christ. It is time for us to discover that the church is the very best place to discover and experience good guilt together and the promise God can bring.

Remember, it starts with us. *Lord Jesus Christ, Son of God, have mercy on us and forgive us our sins. Amen.*

Journal Prompt

- **Reflecting on Repentance's Perception:** How has your view of repentance changed through this book? Do you see it as a life-giving practice or still burdensome? What steps can you take to embrace it for a flourishing life faith?

---

2. Barna, "Self-Described Christians Dominate America but Wrestle with Four Aspects of Spiritual Depth."

CHAPTER 18 | CHURCH: THE BEST PLACE TO REPENT!

As American Christians, we often filter our faith through individualism. When we hear "Repent!" we assume it's a personal call. But scripture teaches that true repentance is the call of entire Christian communities where we not only receive God's forgiveness but also experience transformation together as a single body of believers.

No "Holy Solitaries"

An eye-opening moment in my ministry came when I introduced a confirmation class requiring parents to participate alongside their teens. The response? Visible discomfort. One parent even asked, "But won't talking about faith with our children be awkward?" We've become so convinced that faith is a private/individual matter that even our parents are no longer equipped, nor find it necessary, to discuss faith with their children. We're a church of solitary followers of Jesus. No wonder being a disciple is so challenging. No wonder we balk at the thought of living earnestly repentant lives. We've been conditioned to think we have to do it all alone. There's nothing biblical about that at all.

John Wesley had strong words for those who tried to follow Jesus alone, calling them "Holy Solitaries"—a term he viewed as contradictory to the gospel:

> Solitary religion is not to be found [in the Gospel accounts of Jesus]. "Holy Solitaries" is a phrase no more consistent with the gospel than Holy Adulterers. The gospel of Christ knows of no religion, but social; no holiness but social holiness. Faith working by love, is the length and breadth and depth and height of Christian perfection.[1]

---

1. John Wesley, *Hymns and Sacred Poems (1739)*, ed. Randy L. Maddox, (Durham, NC: Duke Center for Studies in the Wesleyan Tradition, 2020), https://divinity.duke.edu/sites/default/files/documents/04_Hymns_and_Sacred_Poems_%281739%29.pdf.

The call within Methodism for "Social holiness" is not, as many would argue, a call for social justice. While biblical justice is indeed a tenant of Methodism and a worthy pursuit for all Christians, when Wesley talked about social holiness, he talked about brothers and sisters in the Lord walking in faith *together*. Through such social holiness, we can actually live out the biblical call to work out our faith in love and step into "Christian perfection" (i.e., step even deeper into God's house of grace). This social holiness must include an understanding of and willingness to experience social repentance together.

Good Guilt for God's Family

Let's briefly return to the foundational biblical passage for this book from the letter of 1 John. Remember in 1:9 when the pastor assures his congregation, "If we confess our sins, he who is faithful and just will forgive us our sins and cleanse us from all unrighteousness"? Recall the impetus of this passage—the congregation of 1 John was ignoring, to an extreme degree, the reality of sin in their lives. Let me pause and push back on any hesitancy within you to think that you and your church aren't like the church of 1 John. Yes, you and your congregation may not wholly deny that sin has any role in their lives anymore, but I believe there's something like the 1 John congregation within many of our church bodies. Evangelical New Testament scholar I. Howard Marshall made this point as he reflected on this very passage:

> Modern men treat sin lightly [like those in 1 John did], and insofar as they do believe in God, they believe that he makes considerable allowances for our weaknesses and failures. The Message that God is light is not taken with sufficient seriousness. Probably few people would deny that acts of deliberate, clear-cut evil are incompatible with true religion. *What they do deny is that any of their own acts fall into that category.*[2]

The congregations we worship in probably don't openly profess that sin does not affect us at all. Still, we share in the all-too-human temptation to not give the serious threat of present sin in the life of the believing Christian the attention that scripture calls for. So, even as we socially deny sin's significance in our Christian lives, we are called to socially confess, socially repent, and socially experience good guilt together as a family of God.

Let me get nerdy here to help drive home how important this point was for the author of 1 John. The Greek word for "confess" in 1 John 1:9, *homolo-*

---

2. I. Howard Marshall, *The Epistles of John*, New International Commentary on the New Testament (Grand Rapids: William B. Eerdmans Publishing Company, 1978), 120.

gein, doesn't imply private reflection but public agreement with God about our sin and need for grace. *Homologein* is used six times across the letters commonly agreed to be written by the same person (1, 2, and 3 John), and in every other instance, it refers to confessing Christ publicly and together. This connection is intentional. Just as confessing Christ is a public declaration of alignment with Him, confessing our sins is a declaration of our alignment with God's truth about ourselves, and this alignment must happen publicly within the body of Christ.

As suggested in 1 John, social repentance through confession is not about humiliation but humility. It's about standing before your spiritual siblings and saying, "I need God, and I need you to help me follow Him better." It is about allowing your vulnerability to spark renewal, not just in your own life but in the lives of others. And what is the result of such an honest, bold confession? "He who is faithful and just will forgive us our sins and cleanse us from all unrighteousness" (1 John 1:9). The cleansing is not just for the individual but for the community.

Social repentance has sparked revival throughout history from early Methodists confessing in small groups to gospel choir members at Asbury praying the night before revival broke out. People confess together, hear God's assurance of forgiveness together, and then rise renewed together. This is the beauty of God's family in action.

"The Promise is for All of Us"

Here's your challenge: What if your church fully embraced 1 John 1:9 and openly confessed sin together, trusting God to forgive and renew your entire congregation? I believe that, like the church of 1 John, you might find that God does something in your midst that no one could anticipate because there is no limit to what He can do with a humble, repentant family, for He's not only able to forgive your individual sins but also "the sins of the whole world" (1 John 2:2).

As one congregant wrote to me when I asked them to reflect on this very idea: "The promise is for all of us. Not just me. It is for all who love Him and are called according to his purpose—this is our hope." If repentance has a PR problem, we must fix it—not alone but together. The promise is not just for you or me but for all of us. We are called to confess, to trust in God's grace, and to embrace repentance as a family of faith.

Journal Prompt

- **Social Holiness in Practice**: Recall when your faith deepened through a church community experience. How does communal confession and repentance enhance your bond with God and fortify your church family?

CHAPTER 19 | A COMMUNITY HABIT

Bad habits thrive in isolation; good habits flourish in community. Athletes train better in groups. New skills are easier to learn in a class. Recovery lasts longer with accountability. The same is true for repentance; when we practice it together, it becomes a life-giving habit.

The same is true with the habit of opening our lives to the Spirit's conviction of good guilt and stepping into repentant living. By now, I hope you long for a habit of repentance, trusting that it leads to joyful obedience and newness of life. Maybe you've already begun practicing it in daily life. I believe God can and will do many things through our own repentant acts of confession before the Lord; however, I also believe we were created not to go it alone but to practice and form this habit together. And what better way to learn about, practice, and grow in the assurance of what God can do through repentant living than when brothers and sisters gather together for worship each week? Repentance is personal, but it is not supposed to stay private.

In Chapter 4, we briefly looked at the life of King Josiah, a young king in Israel who discovered God's law in the Temple storage facilities. While reading those long-lost words of the Lord, Josiah experienced the same good guilt we have been discussing this whole time (2 Chronicles 34:19-30). He experienced a sense of where he and his people had gone off course. We see good guilt at play when we read that Josiah "tore his clothes" (v 19) over the fact that his people and their ancestors "did not keep the word of the LORD" or done "in accordance with all that is written in this book" (v 21). He didn't shove God's word back in the storage closet. He didn't try to bury what God was doing in his heart. He gave into the good guilt and trusted God's call to be a repentant people.

Josiah "gathered together all the elders of Judah and Jerusalem" (v 29). Soon, "all the people both great and small" joined in (v 30). Together, they repented, worshiped, and celebrated Passover, perhaps for the first time in generations. We can continue in this great tradition as we gather publicly and communally, "all people great and small," to hear God's word read to us, to repent and turn back to God, and to celebrate the new Passover at Christ's table of grace week after week.

Weekly Worship. Weekly Repentance.

As a pastor, I witness the power of weekly worship, and the consequences when people neglect it. Words like *habit/habitual* don't have to mean something mundane or legalistic in our spiritual lives. I hope you have a habit of prayer. I hope you have a habit of reading scripture. I hope you have a habit of weekly worship with the body of Christ. I hope you have habits that reveal a desire to step deeper into God's house of sanctification. So, go to church and worship habitually with your Christian brothers and sisters because, in doing so, among many other things, the very act of choosing to worship is an act of repentance itself.

The world fights against worship. Satan would rather you sleep in, go to brunch, or do anything but gather with God's people. And because I'm human too, those thoughts go through my head (and my heart) just like they do yours. The world wants me to step away from God, and there are so many ways throughout the week that I do just that. Yet on Sundays, God's conviction speaks to me and countless others around the globe every single week to step *back* to God, repent of all the ways my life is pulled toward the world, and choose to seek Him through worship in my local congregation. While the act of choosing to go to worship is indeed repentant, so much more repentance can happen within our worship hours if we only allow it.

When you enter the sanctuary, you can shed your tendency to stay in your comfortable bubble of friends and instead greet a new or unfamiliar face, welcoming them to the church. When you see a song you dislike in the bulletin, don't let selfishness take over. Instead of resenting the music, lean into good guilt and ask God to transform your worship. When tempted to check your phone during a long prayer or sermon, you can choose to refocus your attention on God. Embrace good guilt and remember that God loves to hear and answer your prayers.

When, during a scripture reading or a sermon topic, you think, "Man, this passage (or this sermon) is really going after *those people*," stop and consider how God may not be talking about *those people* but about you. Remember, we're far too good at seeing the sin in someone else's life at the expense of ignoring it in our own, as Jesus observed: "Why do you see the speck in your neighbor's eye, but do not notice the log in your own eye?" (Matthew 7:3). Yes, your pastor may be preaching about someone else's sin, but your pastor is likely preaching about *your* sin as well.

When asked to pray a corporate confession, instead of thinking, "How presumptuous! I haven't done anything like that," allow the Spirit to soften your heart. Say the words and pray, taking a repentant posture rather than a defensive one. This is your time to confess, not argue your case. Such prayers should lead us not to gloom but to hope and promise. Receive the joy-filled freedom offered at the end of such prayers: "...free us for joyful obedience..."

When you're about to come to the communion table, you can choose to look at your watch, thinking that the sermon has already gone on too long and now you're going to be there even longer because it's Communion Sunday. Or you can choose to see this moment as the powerfully repentant moment it promises to be. You, along with your church family, can come to the table of Christ's sacrificed and risen body, earnestly repent your sin together, and joyfully receive God's forgiveness through the life, death, and resurrection of Jesus Christ the Lord!

Our Regular Habits. God's Miraculous Power.

In the early 1800s, northeast of Lexington, Kentucky, a group of Presbyterians held annual "communion gatherings" in a log meeting house. Each summer, hundreds gathered for preaching, singing, and the Lord's Supper. Through this habitual gathering of some 400 or so people each year, God moved powerfully at the dawn of the 19th century.

Then, in August 1801, instead of a few hundred people, 10,000 to 20,000 arrived. Revival had come! That's up to 10% of the entire population of Kentucky at the time in one location over 6 or 7 days. People from surrounding states and further flocked to be part of what God was doing in that place. Revival wasn't the plan. The plan was for the regular habit of a particular group of God's people to proceed normally. Yet, through the regular repentant habits of God's people, God worked His miraculous power. Repentance led to revival and renewal, as the Cane Ridge Revival was the catalyst of the entire 2nd Great Awakening, from which countless lives were saved for the Lord, and social reforms swept the nation that would bring life abundant to millions for generations and generations.

Next time you're tempted to skip church, remember: God works through ordinary habits. Repentance isn't routine—it's an invitation to deeper grace. Your regular habits of repentance as part of a church family can change your individual life, but who knows at what point God will choose to work through your habits to bring His much-needed change to literally tens of thousands?

Journal Prompt

- **Community vs. Individual Growth:** How do your weekly worship practices create space for repentance and renewal? What steps can you take to approach worship as an opportunity for deeper connection with God and others?

CHAPTER 20 | REPENTANCE IS YOUR NEXT MISSION STRATEGY

As our culture shifts to avoid repentance more and more, our churches reflect this avoidance. Faith participation in the U.S. has declined for decades. In 2021, Gallup reported that for the first time in 80 years, fewer than 50% of adults attended worship.[1]

My own tradition of Methodism has not been immune to this hemorrhaging of members. United Methodism, the largest Methodism/Wesleyan denomination in the U.S., lost 3.8 million members in the years leading up to 2022. Regardless of whether a local congregation remained United Methodist, joined the newly formed Global Methodist Church, or remained independent in the recent disaffiliation movement in United Methodism, most of those local congregations likely saw the same thing that I have seen, fewer and fewer people in our congregations.

Church leaders have invested heavily to reverse this decline, but no strategy will work unless we first confront the real issue. Church leadership cannot simply think that the next idea or novel approach will solve all their problems. No new curriculum, consultant, or gimmick will fix this. The answer isn't "the next big thing." The answer is the oldest thing: repentance. The new shiny thing in the marketplace shouldn't be your next mission strategy. Instead, a very old thing, something God has called his people to time and time again, repentant living, can be your next mission strategy. Not only can it be, but I believe it should be.

Discipleship is Mission

John Wesley's Methodism thrived because he never separated evangelism from discipleship. Today, churches divide the two with separate pastors,

1. Jeffrey M. Jones, "U.S. Church Membership Falls Below Majority for First Time," *Gallup* (blog), March 29, 2021, https://news.gallup.com/poll/341963/church-membership-falls-below-majority-first-time.aspx.

books, and sermon series—some dedicated to evangelism, while others are dedicated to discipleship. But Jesus gave one Great Commission not two: "Go therefore and make disciples…" (Matthew 28:19).

When we look at the very first time the church was given a mission statement back in Matthew 28, we see Jesus giving us *one* mission: "Go therefore and make disciples of all nations, baptizing them in the name of the Father and of the Son and of the Holy Spirit" (Matthew 28:19). We don't call this passage the Great Commission*s* (plural) but a single Great *Commission*. Yes, missional efforts must go into reaching and baptizing new believers, but for Jesus, it's all part of "making disciples." And I don't think the making of a disciple is a one-and-done thing. In Jesus' eyes, we are always *becoming* the disciples he calls us to be. A disciple is always becoming, always repenting, always open to the Spirit's conviction, always stepping into abundant life.

John Mark Comer, pastor and author of *Practicing the Way*, champions the need for continual repentance: "*When* you sin (and I will, as you will), don't hide it from God. Hold it before God, with no excuses, no blame shifting, no denial, just utter vulnerability, and let God love you as you *are*. And then let God love you into who you have the potential to *become*."[2] And who is it that we all have the potential to become? A disciple of Christ—a disciple who can then make more and more repentant disciples.

Repentant Disciples Make Repentant Disciples

Picture a disciple who embraces repentance—not as shame but as freedom. They lean into good guilt, knowing it leads to hope. Confession isn't a one-time event; it's a daily return to God's love.

This disciple's life is shaped by repentance. They're not trying to fake it or put on a spiritual performance; they're just real. They've wrestled with their shortcomings, laid them bare before God, and found grace waiting on the other side. That kind of honesty changes you. It clarifies what matters most: God's grace, salvation through faith, and the life we're all invited into. Their words land differently when they speak to a friend over coffee or in a small group setting. They're not just sharing knowledge; they're sharing their journey—what it looks like to be transformed by God's love.

Their lives invite others in. Honest repentance makes space for others to be real. It's not about berating others into faith; it's about modeling transformation. They're proof that confession isn't the end; it's the beginning of

---

2. John Mark Comer, *Practicing the Way* (Colorado Springs, CO: WaterBrook, 2024), 50. Emphasis added.

something new. And that "something new" isn't just for them. It ripples out to everyone they encounter.

This is what a disciple on mission looks like—not someone who *is* perfect but someone who's constantly *being made* perfect in Christ. They live a life of turning and returning, and in doing so, they show others the way. Discipleship isn't a one-and-done deal. It's a lifetime of confession, repentance, and renewal—a rhythm pulling us closer to the abundant life that Jesus promises. And it's that life—a life that's honest, open, and marked by good guilt—that has the power to inspire others to follow Him too.

No church growth strategy can replace the first one: *make disciples*. The making of disciples starts when we begin to take discipleship seriously in our own lives. Every time you gather with your discipleship small group and share your struggles with sin (as early Methodists were not only prone to do but *required* to do), you become more like the disciple you were called to be and thus the disciple-maker God needs you to be. Every time you earnestly repent of your sin before the sacrificed and risen body of Christ at the Lord's Supper, you become more like the disciple you were called to be and thus the disciple-maker God needs you to be. Every time you own up to your mistakes, shortcomings, and sins to God and those you've sinned against, you become more like the disciple you were called to be. I'm convinced that what the world needs to see from the church now more than ever is a church that is not trying to cover up misdeeds or failings but a church that is willing to fall on its knees and say, "I'm sorry" and in doing so, reveal our faith in God's amazing grace to forgive our great sins and heal our brokenness. If that's the message we want the world to hear, believe in, and embrace, we first have to show the world that it's a message we genuinely believe and embrace in our own lives.

Humbled and Sent

Repentance isn't just personal; it's the church's best strategy for renewal. Instead of looking for another church-growth book, what if your mission simply began with repentance? Instead of brushing mistakes under the rug, go to the person you wronged and say, "I'm sorry," and confess your sin before the Lord. Instead of ignoring that invitation to join a discipleship small group where you may need to get vulnerable and honest about your sins, lean into that invitation, join that group, and discover the power of regular repentant living with your brothers and sisters in Christ. Instead of viewing church worship only as a time to feel uplifted, embrace it for what it is: God's invitation to repent from the remaining sin in your life and turn more to Him with each daily step. Imagine you and everyone in your church taking that humble posture of repentance wherever you go—both exemplifying such humble grace in your interactions with others and sharing the undeniable message of hope, promise, and new life that will fill your soul so much that you can't help but tell others about it!

We can't adequately share the Good News of Jesus with the world unless we first remember that we have to believe in it and experience it daily for ourselves. No program, curriculum, or book (certainly not this one) can accomplish this in your life and your church. The only thing that will work for any of our churches is to remember the very first message that Jesus ever preached: "Repent, for the kingdom of heaven has come near" (Matthew 4:17 NIV) and to carry that message with us as we follow Jesus' final message to "make disciples of all nations…" (Matthew 28:19).

Journal Prompt

- **Humbled and Sent**: How can your church create a culture of repentance that speaks to the broader world? What personal steps can you take to foster confession, forgiveness, and grace within your community?

Part V Check-In

As we close Part V, take a moment to reflect on your journey with God this week. This section explored how repentance isn't just personal—it's communal, missional, and transformative. It challenged us to rethink how confession, humility, and discipleship shape not only our individual faith but also our churches and outreach.

Using the scale below, mark where you honestly find yourself: -10 (Distant, burdened by guilt) to +10 (Free, joyful in repentance)

- Where do you land this week and why?
- Have you embraced repentance as a way of life, or does it still feel like something to avoid?
- If you feel distant from God, is there an area of your life where He's inviting you to confess and turn back toward Him?
- What would it look like to practice repentance in community—not just privately, but alongside your church family?
- How can you model a repentant heart to others, showing them that repentance is not shameful but life-giving?

Let this be a moment of honest reflection—God's grace meets us where we are, but He never leaves us there.

Part VI

EMBRACING GOOD GUILT

CHAPTER 21 | "BUT WHAT CAN I DO?"

One of the most enduring spiritual resources of the English-speaking world, *The Book of Common Prayer*, emerged in 16th-century England and remains a guide for daily repentance and prayer. Rather than elaborate on its many virtues, let's focus on one key idea: *common* prayer designed to unite believers in daily repentance. The word "common" does not mean the book is plain, ordinary, or mundane. Instead, as former Archbishop of Canterbury George Carey stated, "The fundamental purpose of celebrating common prayer is this: to help the Church as a whole pray together daily…"[1] At the heart of *The Book of Common Prayer* are prayers of confession and repentance, calling us to open our hearts to healthy guilt and God's forgiveness. Repentance isn't just for pastors or 'super Christians.' It's for all of us—ordinary and common people longing to know God more.

Cultivating Daily Repentance

I'm convinced God created us to thrive on habit. Think about it. God placed us in a world of repetitive cycles: Day and night, a waxing and waning moon, a shifting of seasons, again and again and again. To survive in such cycles, we have to be creatures of habit. Just as it's important to brush our teeth in the morning and at night, it's also important to experience the cleansing of our souls regularly.

Some resist spiritual habits, claiming "I have Jesus, and that's enough." But habits shape us, either drawing us closer to Christ or further away. Winfield Bevins, pastor, professor, and church planter who speaks and writes regularly on spiritual formation, reminds us that "Habits, whether good or bad, have the power to shape our character and mold our will."[2] In other words, if we want to be repentant people, we must practice repentance.

---

1. Winfield Bevins, *Our Common Prayer: A Field Guide to the Book of Common Prayer*, (Hanover, NH: Simeon Press, 2013), 21.

2. Winfield Bevins, *Ever Ancient, Ever New* (Grand Rapids, MI: Zondervan, 2019), 161.

Morning Prayer

Everyone benefits from a morning prayer. Even if you're not a 'morning person,' dedicating your first moments to God is a step of repentance in itself—turning away from just a few more minutes of sleep and turning toward a deeper walk with Christ. Whatever your morning prayer routine, include confession. We learned a simple confessional prayer earlier in the book. It's a prayer I use every single morning:

Lord Jesus Christ, Son of God, have mercy on me, for I have sinned.

I typically pray this slowly three times in a row. Why three? Well, praying in a trinity is never a bad habit for any Christian. But more than that, usually if I'm praying it slowly, by the time I get to the third time through, sins that I hadn't even considered, remembered, or thought of make their way to the surface.

Along with this prayer, you can bring in some tried-and-true prayers of confession from the Psalms:

- "Against you, you alone, have I sinned, and done what is evil in your sight... Create in me a clean heart, O God, and put a new and right spirit within me." (Psalm 51:4, 10)

- "I acknowledged my sin to you, and I did not hide my iniquity; I said, 'I will confess my transgressions to the LORD,' and you forgave the guilt of my sin." (Psalm 32:5)

- "Search me, God, and know my heart; test me and know my anxious thoughts. See if there is any offensive way in me, and lead me in the way everlasting." (Psalm 139:23–24 NIV)

- "My guilt has overwhelmed me like a burden too heavy to bear... LORD, do not forsake me; do not be far from me, my God." (Psalm 38:4, 21 NIV)

Finally, I ensure that any published devotional resources I use include some repentant reflection. No daily time with God should only give you comfort in where you're at; it should stir a holy discontentedness to drive you to be more like Christ. That holy discontent is an experience of good guilt.

A resource where you're sure to find daily guidance in repentant prayer is the aforementioned *Book of Common Prayer*. A favorite of mine, I've probably prayed through the model of daily prayer provided by this book about 70–80% of my days over the past decade. Along with the Holy Spirit conviction that comes from the wide variety of scripture readings that *Common Prayer* will take you through each day, this daily prayer of confession consistently churns up good guilt in my heart:

> Most merciful God, we confess that we have sinned against you in thought, word, and deed, by what we have done, and by what we have left undone. We have not loved you with our whole heart; we have not loved our neighbors as ourselves. We are truly sorry and we humbly repent. For the sake of your Son Jesus Christ, have mercy on us and forgive us; that we may delight in your will, and walk in your ways, to the glory of your Name. Amen.[3]

If you want to try *The Book of Common Prayer*, I encourage you to buy Winfield Bevins's excellent beginner's guide *Our Common Prayer: A Field Guide to the Book of Common Prayer*. You can also start right away by downloading the free app called *My Daily Office* by Manna Software, LLC. ("Office" here is derived from the Latin *officium,* which was originally used to call this type of regular, daily prayer a "divine duty.") However, and whenever you regularly engage with scripture and prayer each day and whatever resources you use, never miss this powerful daily moment between you and God to ask Him to reveal good guilt in your life, confess your sins, turn toward Him in repentance, and receive His assurance of forgiveness.

Midday Checkup

Just as we may check our to-do lists at work throughout the day, why not do the same with God? Pick a midday time and reflect on where your heart has been so far. Make this part of your daily prayer over your lunch each day. Perhaps you're in a location during the lunch hour where you can get up and walk around and with each prayerful step, consider all the steps you have already taken that day. Were they steps of selfishness and pride, or were they steps for Christ? Try revisiting those sins you confessed earlier in the morning. Did they rear their ugly head again? If so, don't wallow in shame and despair. Confess, repent, embrace God's forgiveness, and keep living for Christ! Set an alarm on your watch. Put it on your calendar. Somehow, establish a brief time in the middle of each day to check in with God.

Evening Examen

The regular practice of examining one's day certainly goes back to the early days of the church, but the formal *Daily Examen,* as it is now called, can

---

3. *Book of Common Prayer* (Cambridge, 1770), http://archive.org/details/bookofcommonpray00chur.

be traced back to St. Ignatius of Loyola, who lived more than five hundred years ago. I practice a simple five-step HEART Examen prayer each night, often counting each step on my fingers as I drift to sleep: (1) Honor God's presence; (2) Express thanks; (3) Acknowledge faults; (4) Resolve to obey; (5) Trust God with tomorrow:

1. **Honor God's Presence:** Begin by resting in God's presence. Take a few deep breaths and focus on God's love for you, recalling that He is with you and you are with Him.

2. **Express Thanks:** Reflect on the day's blessings and thank God for specific moments or experiences. Praise Him for the good, even amidst challenges, as evidence of God's grace.

3. **Acknowledge Faults:** Think back over the events of your day. Ask God to reveal moments when you fell short, acted out of selfishness, and failed to live in holiness. This is not a time for self-condemnation but honest self-examination under God's grace. Acknowledge your shortcomings. Identify specific sins— actions, thoughts, or attitudes for which repentance is needed. Bring this to God in prayer, asking for forgiveness.

4. **Resolve to Obey:** Embrace God's forgiveness in your life and commit to stepping even deeper into the new life of joyful obedience that God longs for you to live.

5. **Trust God with Tomorrow:** Close with a short prayer, entrusting the passing day and the future into God's hands. (Example: "Lord, thank you for walking with me today. Help me grow closer to you tomorrow. Amen.")

Just the Beginning of What You Can Do

While the above suggestions only scratch the surface of ways you can incorporate repentant living in your daily life, I believe these practices of morning prayers, midday check-ins, and evening examen will help you begin to cultivate a rhythm of humility and transformation essential for your journey with Christ. These are not just private exercises; they ripple outward, shaping your relationships, attitude, and ability to engage with others in the body of Christ. Repentance is not an isolated act; it's a communal reality. As you practice turning back to God daily, you contribute to a collective openness in your church for revival and renewal. Imagine the power of an entire congregation of believers regularly confessing, repenting, and receiving God's forgiveness—not only as individuals but also as a community. What might God do through a church fully committed to repentance?

Daily repentance in your own life builds the foundation for something greater—corporate repentance and revival. This is the heartbeat of the church at its best: a people united in humility, fully alive in the joy of God's forgiveness, and open to the Spirit's leading. In the next chapter, we'll take a closer look at how you can bring this personal practice into the life of your church, becoming a part of the greater work of repentance in your community. From small group confession to corporate prayers of forgiveness during worship, you'll discover how to move from individual renewal to communal transformation. It's not just about what God is doing in you—it's about what He wants to do through you for His body and kingdom's sake.

Journal Prompt

- **Reflect on Your Habits**: Reflect on your current spiritual habits. Are you intentionally building space for repentance in your daily routine, such as through morning prayer, a midday check-in, or an evening examen? How might incorporating one of these practices bring greater humility, peace, and renewal to your walk with God?

CHAPTER 22 | "NOW, WHAT CAN *WE* DO?"

If this feels too daunting to tackle all alone, that's a good thing! None of us were meant to live a repentant life alone—it's a life we live together. Once again, if we look at that ancient letter to our now-familiar first-century church, 1 John, we see their pastor is not just calling them to practice confessionally repentant practices in the silence and privacy of their hearts. He calls them to practice such repentance together and publicly.

1 John 1:9 promises, "If we confess our sins, he who is faithful and just will forgive us…." Recall that the Greek word for 'confess' (*homologein*) refers to not only a private confession of the person of Jesus but also a very public confession of Jesus Christ in the presence of God's gathered people. It's clear that to the pastor writing 1 John, confession, either of Jesus or of sin, is not something relegated to private silence, but a vital part of what God's people do when they gather together. So, along with the personal practices of repentant living, I pray you're feeling God's call to add communal and public confessions to your life. Such corporate practices of repentance where the Holy Spirit can walk us through sanctifying experiences of good guilt are foundational to what it means for Christ followers to live the holy lives He calls us to live.

Accountable Small Groups

In Global Methodism, there appears to be a burgeoning desire to rediscover the power of accountable small groups, something long neglected yet essential for church renewal. Early Methodism thrived on small groups (Classes and Bands) regularly inviting believers to experience good guilt.

As we've already explored in a previous chapter, questions like "how is it with your soul?", "do you have any sins to confess?", and "do you have anything you are keeping secret?" all cut straight to the bone of our spiritual lives. Yes, these questions may feel daunting, but if we care about the faithful Gospel witness within Methodism, accountable small groups are essential for lasting fruitfulness. Dr. George Hunter (Wesleyan mission and

123

evangelism expert) points out this necessity while recalling an observation made to him by North Korean Pastor Dr. Byounghoon Kang after he had visited some American Methodist churches, saying: "From what I could tell, Methodism does not really exist in America… your Methodist churches do not have class meetings, your people do not minister to each other through class meetings… [Korean] members' involvement in class meetings is even more important than their involvement in Sunday worship. Can there be real Methodism without class meetings?"[1]

If you're not in such a group, prayerfully consider getting in one sooner rather than later. Regularly evaluating the state of your soul within such groups will be a better balm for your soul than you ever knew you needed. If you're a church member, go to your pastor and ask about getting in such a group or getting such groups started at your church. If you're a pastor, what are you waiting for? Get in a group yourself and get some Classes and/or Bands started at your congregation. Some great starting points for laity and clergy are:

The Band Meeting by Kevin Watson and Scott Kisker
The Class Meeting by Kevin Watson
Rediscovering Discipleship: Making Jesus' Final Words our First Work by Robby Gallaty

(In this book, Gallaty takes the Wesleyan model of Classes and Bands and adapts it for non-Methodist contexts).

Prayers of Confession in Worship

Early Methodists couldn't imagine worship without corporate confession. When Wesley was accused by his critics of abandoning the regular custom of corporate prayers for English worshipers (as found in *The Book of Common Prayer*), which is in and of itself an accusation of abandoning confessional prayers, Wesley responded by asserting that "In every parish where I have been curate yet, I have observed the rubrics [of worship] with a scrupulous exactness."[2]

Wesley wasn't innovating; he was restoring scriptural holiness, as seen in both Testaments. When Wesley read passages like 1 John 1:8–2:2 (his favorite book of the Bible, by the way) he saw an example of a pastor yearning for his church to confess their sins and to do so corporately. Wesley led likewise.

---

1. George G. Hunter, *The Recovery of a Contagious Methodist Movement* (Abingdon Press, 2012), 15.

2. John Wesley, "An Earnest Appeal to Men of Reason and Religion," in *John Wesley*, ed. Albert C. Outler (New York, NY: Oxford University Press, 1964), 414.

Does your church confess sin together weekly in worship? Whether through written prayers from a bulletin, a screen, or a hymnal/prayer book or through your pastor guiding you in confession in a more informal way, either way the entire congregation is called to a place of repentance. Pastors, are you doing this? Laity, do you need to set up a meeting with your pastor to ask them about this? The Korean pastor previously mentioned wondered if Methodism can exist without accountable small groups. I wonder if true Christian worship can happen if confession of sin hasn't taken place.

"Constant" Communion

Wesley saw frequent communion as essential for sanctification and deeper life in God's grace. Wesley didn't just advocate for 'frequent' communion—he insisted on 'constant' communion as the bare minimum for a sanctified life: "I say *constantly* receiving [communion]; for as to the phrase of frequent communion, it is absurd to the last degree."[3] And if you recall a previous chapter, "constant" communion for early Methodists always meant "constant" confession and repentance—a constant willingness to experience good guilt.

How *constant* is the practice of communion in your church? If you're a Methodist congregation, it's likely once a month. When you have communion at your church, are you praying a prayer of confession together before coming to the table? If you don't use a formal communion liturgy, does your pastor guide you in a time of reflective confession before communion is served? This is not a matter of me being picky about the order of worship around the communion table. This is a matter of biblical obedience: "Examine yourselves, and only then eat of the bread and drink of the cup" (1 Corinthians 11:28). As a pastor, I know we can be so preoccupied with getting the worship service in under that 60-minute mark that we're willing to omit even the briefest moments from the service to save on time, moments like a simple prayer of confession. Let's not sacrifice repentant worship on the altar of the almighty clock.

And let's not only strive to confessional prayer together at communion, but let's endeavor to come to the communion table *constantly*! Pastors, what would it look like for you to move your church from once-a-month communion to weekly communion? Church members, are you willing to have a pastor who walks you through such a change? Or are you willing and able to ask your pastor why you don't have communion each week in your church?

---

3. John Wesley, "The Duty of Constant Communion," in *John Wesley*, ed. Albert C. Outler (New York, NY: Oxford University Press, 1964), 337.

These are all critical conversations and vital changes we should bring to our lives of worship together.

Testify!

There was a time when testimonies were central to worship—where believers regularly shared how God had moved in their lives. Many of these testimonies certainly involved a person's spiritual growth through acts of repentance. There's great power in the spoken testimony. The book of Revelation reveals this power by pulling back the curtain and showing us just how powerful such testimony is when we're told that those oppressed by the darkness of the evil one "have conquered him by the blood of the Lamb *and by the word of their testimony...*" (Revelation 12:11, emphasis added). The Christian testimony is one of light over darkness, of life conquering death, and of forgiveness erasing sin. We need regular public testimonies of such forgiveness in our worship services. If you want to see revival come to your community, then work to create a culture where the testimony of forgiven sin is the norm. Such testimonies have sparked renewal and revival in communities worldwide throughout the history of the the church. It's happened many times before, and it can happen again, even in your congregation.

Pastors, set an example. Don't be afraid to seek discernment from the Spirit on how you can testify to your own victories over sin through repentance in your sermons. Laity, after over 20 chapters of talking about repentance (and even more journal questions poking and prodding you to consider how you can repent of your sin more and more), do you have a testimony of conquered sin that you can share with your pastor? In doing so, ask if you can share your testimony with the church. Share with your congregation your own fruitful experience of good guilt and allow the Holy Spirit to reveal to all how you've been saved by the blood of the lamb and the power of your testimony.

Preach on Repentance

Pastors, your sermons are some of your greatest discipleship tools. Are you directing them toward repentant living? My preaching professor from Asbury Seminary challenged us that a sermon is not a sermon if it doesn't have a few specific things, and one criterion was that the sermon had to address some particular sin(s) of Christians and/or the church. Challenge yourselves to call out specific sin(s) in every sermon you preach and in doing so, never forget to offer the promise of God's forgiveness through Christ.

But don't just make repentance a part of your sermons. Actually preach on the topic of repentance. I hope I've given you enough biblical, historical, and theological material in this book to help you do that. You can always reach out to me through Invite Ministries, and I promise to help you however I can to get this message coming from your pulpit and into your congregation. If Pastors want to see their congregations grow more and more repentant and thus more holy, then congregations must see such repentant living coming from their pastors. For most of us, that starts with the sermons we preach week after week.

A Call to Action for the Church

It's time for the church to reclaim repentance. Confession isn't occasional or private; it's a shared, transformative act that prepares us for God's grace. As a body of believers, we must create spaces where the conviction of sin is not feared but embraced as an invitation to live more deeply in Christ.

To church leaders (staff, volunteers, laity, and clergy alike), it begins with us. Let us model the humility of confession from the pulpit and in our personal lives. Integrate confession prayers into worship, guide congregations through corporate repentance, and preach boldly on the necessity of a repentant life. Likewise, every member of Christ's body has a role to play. Seek accountability, speak truth in love, and share testimonies of God's grace in overcoming sin.

Journal Prompt

- **Confession in Community**: Consider how your church practices repentance—worship, testimonies, small groups, etc. What can you do to foster a culture of confession and accountability? How could these changes promote deeper renewal for individuals and the church?

CHAPTER 23 | THE JOURNEY AHEAD

My son is in driver's ed, excited yet nervous, just as I was at his age. At first, remembering everything—hands at 10 and 2, checking mirrors, using turn signals—felt overwhelming. But with practice, those habits became second nature. The same is true for repentance. At first, self-examination may seem exhausting, but over time, it becomes a natural rhythm of faith.

Maybe you were thankful for the past few chapters on the practical steps you and your congregation can take to become the repentant people God calls you to be. Maybe you're convinced that good guilt is a good thing in your life of faith. However, some, if not many, may think this is all too much. Maybe you're still wondering how such a life can be a blessing and how this could be anything but despairing and shame-ridden.

Many see repentance like a backseat driver yelling at them to look in the mirrors constantly. But safe driving—and faithful living—requires both looking ahead and checking the rearview mirror. I'm not here to make you obsess over the past but to encourage you that regular mirror-checking in the form of self-examination strengthens your faith.

At first, the call for you to practice a life of repentance may feel overwhelming, as if there's just too much to look at in your rear-view mirrors each day to consider what has happened that you need to confess to the Lord. But just like examining your mirrors when you drive today is second nature so is the life of the repentant believer. The more you do it, the more "driving hours" you put in, the more you'll not only become proficient in looking back, but you'll also become the driver—the disciple—that God has called you to be, and you'll be amazed at how natural it actually is.

Metanoia: Looking Back to Move Forward

The Greek word *metanoia* is often used for "repentance" in our Bibles. The root words used here, *meta* ("after") and *nous* ("mind, understanding"), lead to a literal translation of "change your mind," and it's sadly becoming common in some Christian circles to argue that biblical repentance *only* means a "change of mind" (rather than the significance of what a *transformed* mind actually is). While that's part of the meaning, relying on this definition alone risks enabling us to move away from calling out any sinful behavior. I get it. "Change your mind" sounds much more palatable than "repent." But this move to sugar-coat biblical repentance is doing more harm than good. And it's also unnecessary. This reframing often comes when we think that calls to repent will turn people off and turn people away. But remember, biblical repentance is not the call to shame and self-flagellation as many think it is.

Changing our minds absolutely happens in repentance, but when scoping the biblical texts from Genesis to Revelation, we see that biblical repentance, a biblical "changing of one's mind," means a "moral turn of the whole person from sin and to God."[1] To use our driving analogy again, being able to turn left or right is not enough to be considered a good driver, just like being able to "change one's mind" is not enough to consider yourself a faithful follower of Jesus. We must be well practiced and convinced that a regular look in our rear mirrors (i.e., a willingness to honestly self-examine and realize our past sins) is the only way to keep moving forward in our life of faith.

And what should we be looking for as we self-examine? New Testament expert Dr. Jonathan Lunde concisely defines sin as "anything that offends or hinders one's relationship" with God and should thus "be parted with."[2] It's a simple definition on paper, but understanding those things that offend and hinder our relationship with God is, for most of us, part of the life-long journey of discipleship. I believe God is immensely faithful in revealing those places in our lives that we need to repent of, even as we are faithful in drawing nearer to Him through prayer, study, worship, and service as part of the body of Christ. So, keep worshiping with your church, praying to your God, serving as the hands and feet of Jesus, and studying the scriptures. As we do all these things and grow in Christ, His Word helps us identify areas needing repentance. Here are some passages that reveal what offends or hinders our relationship with God.

Old Testament Passages

1. Exodus 20:1–17 (The Ten Commandments)
   - These commands are a great place to start reflecting on our lives. They address sins such as idolatry, dishonesty, jealousy, and a lack of respect for God and others.

---

1. William D. Mounce, *Mounce's Complete Expository Dictionary of Old and New Testament Words* (Grand Rapids, MI: Zondervan, 2006), 581.

2. Jonathan Lunde, "Repentance," in *Dictionary of Jesus and the Gospels*, ed. Joel B. Green, Scot McKnight, and I. Howard Marshall (Downers Grove, IL: InterVarsity Press, 1992), 671.

2. Psalm 51:1–17 (David's Prayer of Repentance)

   ○ David's raw and honest confession of sin offers a model for us to examine our own hearts and ask for God's cleansing and renewal.

3. Isaiah 59:1–8 (The Consequences of Sin)

   ○ This passage calls out social and relational sins like injustice, dishonesty, and violence, reminding us how sin creates distance between us and God.

New Testament Passages

1. Matthew 5:21–48 (The Sermon on the Mount)

   ○ The entire Sermon on the Mount in Matthew 5–7 should be regularly read and prayerfully considered by disciples throughout their lives as a way of self-examination and repentant living. In this specific passage, Jesus goes beyond outward actions (like murder and adultery) to challenge us to examine our inner attitudes—things like anger, lust, and holding grudges.

2. Mark 7:20–23 (The Heart as the Source of Sin)

   ○ Jesus makes it clear that sin starts in the heart, listing examples like evil thoughts, greed, deceit, and pride. It's an invitation to examine what's going on inside us.

3. Romans 1:28–32 (The Depravity of Humanity)

   ○ Paul outlines a thorough list of sins, including envy, gossip, arrogance, and disobedience to parents, inviting us to examine patterns that might be lurking in our lives.

4. 1 Corinthians 6:9–11 (Sins that Bar Entry to God's Kingdom)

   ○ This passage provides a sobering list of sins (like sex outside of the monogamous marriage of a male and female, idolatry, greed, and drunkenness) but ends with the hopeful reminder of God's power to transform us.

5. Galatians 5:19–26 (Works of the Flesh)

   ○ Paul contrasts sinful behaviors like jealousy, selfish ambition, and fits of rage with the fruits of the Spirit, urging us to reflect on what kind of fruit our lives bear.

6. James 3:1–12 (Sins of the Tongue)

   ○ Words have incredible power, and James challenges us to reflect on how we use them, either to build others up or to tear them down.

Treat the above passages and all of scripture as a way of examining your past way of living, either the way you lived 5 minutes or 5 years ago. If you see in these passages places of your life where you've been unrepentant, don't ignore that conviction! Let God work through that good guilt, repent of that way of living, receive His forgiveness through Jesus Christ on the cross, and step into the new hope and promise that God longs for you to know! Let these passages be the rear-view mirror of your life. Regularly look at them. At first, it may seem too much to do, remember, and process. But over time, it will become second nature, and you'll discover how vital it is to check your mirrors as you continue to drive forward on the path of Christ before you.

Live the Promise

Jesus never promised an easy life. He said, "In this world you will have trouble" (John 16:33 NIV). One of those challenges is choosing holiness—honest self-reflection, confession, and truth—when the world prefers avoidance and denial. Jesus is honest about life's troubles but also full of promise: "But take heart! I have overcome the world" (John 16:33 NIV). Hope increases when we see repentance not as a burden, but as the path to greater joy and freedom in Christ. You and I can discover more and more how to live through the experience of good guilt and joyously reach the other side each time, and in doing so, grow more and more oriented to our comforter, redeemer, friend, and Lord. Jesus has indeed overcome the world; it's time we embrace Jesus' victorious life as our own.

Journal Prompt

- **Looking in the Rear-View Mirror:** Jesus said, "Take heart! I have overcome the world." How does this shape your view of self-examination and repentance? As you reflect on areas where God might be asking you to examine your life, how does Christ's assurance encourage you to face those truths with hope?

CHAPTER 24 | GOOD GUILT. GREAT JOY. REVIVAL READY!

Cultural analyst Aaron Renn believes we live in a "negative world." He means that American culture has, by and large, a negative view of Christianity, and the U.S. is a place where "Christian morality is expressly repudiated…"[1] It's easy to look outside our churches and lives and nod our heads in agreement with Renn's assessment. It's quite another thing to look at ourselves and realize that we too are likely living lives that, in many ways, are just as out of line with the ways of Jesus as our culture. Far too many sinful behaviors and postures are now acceptable, excusable, and justifiable in the day-to-day lives of Americans, self-professing Christians included. What's Renn's answer? First and foremost, he says, we need to "examine ourselves, consider our ways, count the cost, and commit to denying ourselves…," and if we don't do this, "nothing else we do will ultimately be of any consequence."[2]

Good guilt leads to transformation. Repentance opens the door to joy and renewal. The challenge above (to "examine ourselves, consider our ways, and commit to denying ourselves") is precisely where revival begins—not in some sweeping cultural program or strategy, but in the humble, everyday repentance from individuals and churches turning back to God. This is where lives are changed, churches are renewed, and communities are prepared for the revival God is eager to bring.

The Personal Revival Pathway

Revival is within reach. Salvation isn't just about stepping inside God's house; it's about exploring its fullness. Too many stop at the door when God invites us deeper into His house.

Daily repentance fuels personal revival. Begin with prayer, reflect throughout the day, and end with self-examination. This isn't about fear or

---

1. Aaron M. Renn, *Life in the Negative World* (Grand Rapids, MI: Zondervan, 2024), 7.

2. Renn, *Life in the Negative World*, 61–62.

shame. It's about trusting God to free you from sin. Remember, if we say we do not sin, we make God a liar (1 John 1:8). Still, if we long to be freed from that sin, all it takes is the humility to admit that sin is there in the first place, for "if anybody does sin, we have an advocate with the Father—Jesus Christ, the Righteous One. He is the atoning sacrifice for our sins, and not only for ours but also for the sins of the whole world" (1 John 2:1–2 NIV).

Revisit all those journal entries you've done and incorporate them into your regular life of prayer and devotion to God. Those sins God has pointed out to you, don't ignore them. Allow God's good guilt, His "godly sorrow," to be active in your life so that you may be led further into His salvation (2 Corinthians 7:9–10 NIV). Be ever aware of those moments in your day when that guilt starts to bubble up. Don't ignore it. Don't brush it aside. Recognize it for the movement from the Spirit that it is—the conviction to tell a friend you're sorry, admit your mistake to your coworker, apologize to your spouse or child, and confess your sin to God. Walking the path of repentance will not lead you to shame and despair. The path of true repentance only goes in one direction: to revival!

The Revival-Ready Church

Revival may begin with repentant individuals, but it spreads through the church. Congregations, like people, must confront their sins. Your commitment to repentance could be the spark that ignites renewal in your church and community.

Josiah repented, and Israel turned back to God. Peter repented, and Jesus called him to lead. John Wesley repented, and Methodism ignited. Revival doesn't begin with strategy; it begins with a humbled heart. A revival-ready church is what God longs for in the world, and God will work through your individual choice to be part of a repentant congregation to make your church ready for such revival.

Don't ignore your pastor's and church's calls to repentance. When the church prays a prayer of confession together in worship, truly pray it! Those prayers can be so much more than words on a page or screen; they can be life-giving words that the Spirit works through to bring freedom and hope to your life.

When communion is celebrated at your church, don't skip over the prayer of confession. Confession and communion are not separate things; confession is part of our holy communion with God through the bread and cup of Christ. There are two requirements to come to God's table: an earnest repentance from sin and a longing to draw closer to the Father through the Son. Don't underestimate God's ability to overcome and wash away your greatest sin with His greater power of love and grace in your life.

Do not fear God's call on your life to band together with other disciples in small groups for the purpose of confession and accountability. Find the people in your church with whom you can share your soul, confess your sin, and admit your desires to keep things secret from God. We need that holy poking and prodding in our lives. And speaking from years of experience as part of such a group, while the feeling of good guilt is always there, it never leads to shame and despair. God *always* works through my honest confession to my band of Christian brothers to bring hope not just to me but to us all!

Recall that in 1949, a small group of Christians on the Hebrides islands off the coast of Scotland banded together within the walls of their church for repentant devotion and expectant prayer to God, and from that, revival broke out. Revival wasn't ignited by this or that person calling out sinners with a bullhorn on the Scottish street corners. No, God blessed the Hebrides with revival when God saw His people, the church, turning back to Him in new ways. It wasn't a new program or curriculum that brought revival.

Remember also what took place the night before God's outpouring of love and grace upon Hughes Auditorium in Wilmore, KY at Asbury University in the winter of 2023. No one went into chapel the day of the outpouring thinking, "Today's the day where we're going to start a revival." No, the story began the night before with a few of Asbury University's Gospel Choir members experiencing the good guilt of godly sorrow through biblical repentance and lament over the true horrors of what humankind is capable of. These Gospel Choir members then went to choir practice which itself felt different that night, in preparation for leading worship in chapel the next day—the day of the outpouring. Renewal, hope, and promise at Asbury University didn't come because of some brand new, energetic personality. It didn't launch due to new or fresh teaching. It wasn't after a new building or strategic plan was launched. None of those things make a revival-ready body of Christ. Revival rises when God's people repent.

The Ripple Effect—Revival Beyond the Church Walls

Peter repented, and revival swept through Jerusalem. Paul repented, and the gospel spread across the Mediterranean. The Moravians repented, launching a 100-year prayer movement that sent missionaries worldwide. Revival is always born in repentance. Some of those Moravian missionaries would meet a young man named John Wesley, and after God strangely warmed his heart to repentance at one of those Moravian prayer meetings, a movement was launched through which God has changed my life, and the lives of countless others over the course of three centuries. And Methodism, like many Christian movements in the Western World, is at a crossroads. We can either continue living into our century-long malaise of living more according to the world and less according to God's holy ways, or we can repent together, turn back to Him in all the ways we can, and be the conduits by which God ushers in another era of world-wide revival.

That vision shouldn't daunt us. It should inspire us. It should motivate us to be ambassadors for such a vision in our own corners of this vast world. Each of those people mentioned above and all of the examples I've shared in this book weren't people who stepped out of their beds one day knowing they would make world-transforming choices for the Lord. No, they stepped out of bed simply choosing to live their day for God right where they were. Your example of holy living—which must include repentant living, in front of your family, your neighbors, your coworkers, at the grocery store check-out counter, at the pharmacy, where you get your tires changed, and everywhere in between—is just the sort of witness God calls each of us to. You represent the greatest news in the history of the cosmos! Exemplify the difference that Good News has made in your own life and is still making. Prayerfully discern what you can do in your own congregation to remind your whole church of this great call on your collective life of faith together. Only God knows how the repentant choices you and our congregations make today will spread His amazing grace across the face of the planet in the future.

Turn to the Father

As a boy, one winter day, I was outside with my dad as he was working on his pickup truck. While he had stepped away, I started playing with one of his tools and broke it. Scared, I ran away. I was certain that there was no point in ever returning home. I was determined to live by a little creek bed next to our property for the rest of my life. After what felt like forever (now I'm sure it was maybe 5–10 minutes total), it dawned on me that my only hope was to return home. Sullen and afraid, I wondered how my dad would react. Would he be mad? Would I get yelled at? I had taken something of his, treated it poorly, and destroyed it. Surely this wouldn't end well for me.

As I approached my dad, now back by his truck, he didn't yell. He didn't look mad at all. He saw the tears on my face as I ran to him and face-planted my tiny body into his loving arms. That was my repentant moment, and he knew it. There was an understanding between us that I knew what I had done was wrong, and in that moment, I realized that running away from that mistake wasn't the answer. Running toward my father was the only path to hope, promise, and a closer relationship with my dad.

The most powerful part of that memory was the words my dad spoke to me as he looked me in my tearful eyes: "Kelly, are you okay?" He didn't chastise me or cast me out for my wrongdoing. All he wanted was for me to be okay. That reassurance would have never come had I stuck to my plan to run away. I only had that experience because I was willing to face the reality of my mistake and return to my father.

My life of following Jesus, studying the scriptures, worshiping with my church family, and prayerfully discerning God's best will for my life has convinced me that one of the most essential gifts that any Christ-follower can offer the world is their own walk of repentance. As the world sees a church that can self-reflect, own its mistakes, and place trust in God for forgiveness, the world will see more of Jesus Christ. We can trust that just as repentance worked to get us into heaven, repentance still works to get more of heaven into us today, like a long-lost, but now found, treasure that still has deep, transformative meaning and value in our lives. We who have experienced this book together and begun this journey of repentance now have tools to continue honestly examining who we are called to be in Christ and what we have done or may still be doing that is keeping us from living out that call. When we humble ourselves to the ways we've failed to be an obedient church we don't have to confront a god to be afraid of. We are promised a heavenly Father who gets down on our level, looks us in the eyes, welcomes us home, and wants us to be okay. We only need to turn to Him.

A church member once told me how they felt after recently considering their own sin, trusting the conviction of good guilt in their life, and receiving forgiveness and pardon from God. They simply said, "I feel freer, more than ever!" Embrace the Spirit's conviction in your life. Embrace good guilt as the body of Christ together. Repent in your life and repent with your church. Never again brush your sins aside as if they had never happened, for we deceive ourselves and make God a liar by living in this way. Step through good guilt with God's help and receive the forgiveness of our advocate and atoning sacrifice, Jesus Christ. In doing so, *feel freer, more than ever!* You are free to be part of God's renewal and revival in your life and your church.

Journal Prompt

- **Live It Out:** As you reflect on your life, your church, and your community, where might repentance—whether in your daily habits, your church's openness to past mistakes, or your interactions with others—create space for God's renewal and revival?

What intentional steps can you take this week to live out the freedom and joy of a repentant life in both personal and communal ways?

Part VI Check-In

As we close Part VI, take a moment to reflect on your journey of repentance. Consider where you are right now in your walk with God.

Using the scale below, mark where you honestly find yourself: -10 (Distant, burdened by guilt) to +10 (Free, joyful in repentance)

- Where do you land this week and why?
- If you feel stuck or weighed down, what's keeping you there? Is there a sin, regret, or fear you need to bring before the Lord?
- If you long to grow toward freedom and joy, what's holding you back? What step of faith or surrender could move you forward?
- If you're experiencing renewal, what led you there? How can you keep embracing repentance as a pathway to revival in your life and church?

This is your moment to honestly reflect. God's grace never leaves you where you are—He calls you deeper into His transforming love. Will you step forward?

DISCUSSION GUIDES

A Note to Group Leaders

Your role is to create a safe, encouraging space where participants can engage with repentance in hope of renewal and joy. Each week builds on the truth that repentance is not a burden of shame but a gift that draws us closer to God and one another.

Leading the Sessions:

- Start with prayer & the opening question to build trust and cultivate reflection.

- Lead by example: share your own reflections to encourage openness.

- Use the chapter specific questions to explore biblical, historical, and theological themes, guiding the group toward recalling and processing the material they've read.

- Be sensitive to the Spirit. Some discussions may bring up guilt or sorrow. Remind participants that godly sorrow leads to joy and transformation not condemnation. Be aware of when to pause the conversation or postpone discussion of a particular struggle someone is having until someone trained (a therapist, counselor, or pastor) may be able to step in to help that individual.

- Encourage action—help participants take practical steps toward personal and communal renewal.

Above all, have an eye toward hope. Repentance is a journey of grace, not worldly perfection, leading to deeper joy, renewal, and intimacy with God.

WEEK 1 GROUP DISCUSSON

Opening Prayer and Icebreaker

- *Open with Prayer*. Ask God to help the group see repentance not as shame but as a pathway to joy.

- *Opening Question*: Share about something you rediscovered after losing it for a long time (an object, a skill, or a hobby). How did it feel to find it again?

Opening Reflections

- What stood out most to you from Chapters 1–4?

- Did a story, scripture, or idea challenge or change your perspective on repentance?

- What most surprised you about the idea of repentance as a gift? Does this challenge your assumptions?

Chapter Specific Reflections

- *Chapter 1*: Revival often begins with repentance. Reflect on the Asbury Outpouring or King Josiah's story. Why do you think repentance creates space for God to renew us?

- *Chapter 2*: The lost and found watch analogy reminds us repentance still "works." What spiritual practices in your life feel forgotten but worth rediscovering?

- *Chapter 3*: God designed us to heal physically and spiritually. How do you see His mercy in creating a way for repentance to be part of that healing process?

- *Chapter 4*: Kelly's story highlights how repentance can free us from bitterness and bring peace. How does his experience shape your view of repentance?

Take Action

- Identify one "lost" spiritual practice or habit you'd like to rediscover this week. Commit to exploring it daily, whether through prayer, scripture, or journaling. Share with the group what one action you feel God might be inviting you to rediscover? Share how you think this could bring you closer to Him?

Closing Prayer and Encouragement

- Close with prayer: Thank God for His mercy and the gift of repentance.

- Encourage the group: Repentance can feel daunting, but it's God's pathway to freedom, healing, and renewal. Let's trust Him and take this journey step by step.

WEEK 2 GROUP DISCUSSION

Opening Prayer and Icebreaker

- *Open with Prayer*: Ask God to reveal His grace through confession and to remove any fear of being honest.

- *Opening Question*: When have you found unexpected relief or clarity after being honest about something?

Opening Reflections

- What resonated most with you from Chapters 5–8?

- Were there any examples or scriptures that shifted your view of confession?

- The book describes repentance as a step toward renewal not shame. What was most encouraging to you about this way to view repentance?

Chapter Specific Questions

- *Chapter 5*: How does seeing the prodigal son's story as relevant for believers shift your understanding of repentance?

- *Chapter 6*: Jesus as our advocate removes fear of isolation. How does this truth encourage you in moments of guilt?

- *Chapter 7*: Positive Psychology connects humility and self-examination to flourishing. How does this align with biblical repentance?

- *Chapter 8*: Communion is described as a means of renewal through confession. How could this deepen your connection to God's grace?

Take Action

- This week, take a small step toward integrating confession into your daily or weekly rhythm. For example, set aside five minutes each evening to reflect and confess to God. Share with the group how this practice might impact your relationship with God.

Closing Prayer and Encouragement

- Close in prayer: Thank God for His grace and invite Him to guide the group in repentance and renewal.

- Encourage the group: Remind the group that repentance is a gift, drawing us closer to God and unlocking His joy and renewal.

WEEK 3 GROUP DISCUSSION

Opening Prayer and Icebreaker

- *Open with Prayer:* Ask God to help the group embrace godly sorrow that leads to transformation and reject worldly shame.

- *Opening Question*: Before reading this book, what do you think your initial response would have been to words like "guilt" and "shame"?

Opening Reflections

- What resonated most with you from Chapters 9–12?

- Words like "guilt," "sorrow," and "repentance" often carry negative connotations. How has this week's reading redefined these terms for you?

- Godly sorrow is described as transformational, while worldly sorrow can feel like a trap. Have you ever experienced either? How did it impact your spiritual journey?

Chapter Specific Questions

- *Chapter 9*: How does distinguishing between guilt ("I did something bad") and shame ("I am bad") change how you approach repentance?

- *Chapter 10*: Reflect on a biblical example of guilt leading to renewal (e.g., Peter, Isaiah). How does their story encourage you to embrace guilt as an invitation to transformation?

- *Chapter 11*: Paul contrasts godly sorrow with worldly sorrow in 2 Corinthians 7:10. How can godly sorrow draw you closer to God and lead to genuine repentance?

- *Chapter 12*: Repentance is described as a journey toward holiness that brings joy. Have you experienced joy after repentance? What contributed to that joy?

Take Action

- This week, consider setting aside a specific time to journal about one area of your life where you feel godly sorrow. Write down how you could invite God's grace to transform that area. Share with the group how this action step either challenges or encourages you.

Closing Prayer and Encouragement

- Close in prayer: Thank God for His grace and the renewal offered through repentance.

- Encourage the group: Remind the group that repentance is a gift from God that draws us closer to His joy and flourishing.

WEEK 4 GROUP DISCUSSION

Opening

- *Open with Prayer*: Pray for wisdom to see how communal repentance can foster renewal.

- *Opening Question*: What's a habit or practice your church has rediscovered that has brought new energy or joy?

Opening Reflections

- What stood out most to you from Chapters 13–16? Was it a historical example, theological insight, or practical suggestion?

- How does your church currently practice communal repentance (e.g., confession or communion)? What might it look like to embrace such practices more deeply?

- Wesley transitioned from "doing" repentance to "being" a repentant person grounded in grace. How does this resonate with your spiritual journey?

Chapter Specific Questions

- *Chapter 13*: Reflect on a time you felt assurance of God's forgiveness, as Wesley did at Aldersgate. How did it transform your outlook or practices?

- *Chapter 14*: The house of salvation metaphor encourages deeper steps into God's grace through repentance. Where do you see yourself—on the porch, at the door, or exploring the rooms? What's your next step?

- *Chapter 15*: Have you ever experienced joy or renewal after confessing sin? How can your group or church create spaces for communal confession to foster this sweetness of repentance?

- *Chapter 16*: American Methodism moved away from practices like constant communion and confession. Do you think these should be reintroduced? What steps might your church take to reclaim them?

Take Action

- As a group, brainstorm one communal act of repentance (e.g., a time of group confession during worship). Do you do this regularly as a congregation? What steps could you take to help your whole church embrace this type of repentance? What other practical steps can a church take together to experience the sort of communal repentance that can lead to renewal and revival?

Closing Prayer and Encouragement

- Close in prayer: Thank God for the gift of repentance and its power to lead to joy and transformation. Pray for guidance toward personal and communal revival.

- Encourage the group: Repentance leads us deeper into God's grace and holiness not shame. Embrace it as a gift that unlocks joy and flourishing for both individuals and the church.

WEEK 5 GROUP DISCUSSION

Opening:

- *Open with Prayer.* Ask God to help the group see repentance as not just personal but as a way to transform communities.

- *Opening Question*: Share a time in your life when facing a hard truth about yourself or your community led to positive change.

Opening Reflections:

- What stood out from Chapters 17–20? Did anything challenge or inspire you?

- Do you see repentance as a practical way to address struggles in your church? Why or why not?

- How does the idea of repentance as a "mission strategy" inspire or challenge you?

Chapter Specific Questions:

- *Chapter 17:* How has negative perceptions of repentance affected your willingness to embrace it? How can you model repentance as an ambassador for Christ?

- *Chapter 18*: Does your church foster communal repentance? How might practicing social repentance deepen your faith and unity as a congregation?

- *Chapter 19*: How does viewing weekly worship as a habit of repentance challenge or affirm your perspective on Sunday services? What can your church learn from King Josiah's story?

- *Chapter 20*: How could repentance as a mission strategy reshape your church's approach to outreach? What role can you play in fostering this shift?

Take Action

- Identify one way you can model repentance as an ambassador of Christ in your community this week, such as through an apology or a reconciliatory act toward another person. Discuss as a group how this sort of action can actually be a mission strategy for your church.

Closing Prayer and Encouragement:

- Close in prayer: Thank God for the gift of repentance and ask for courage to embrace it personally and communally.

- Encourage the group: Remind the group that repentance leads to renewal and revival. Encourage each person to take one step toward living out repentance this week.

WEEK 6 GROUP DISCUSSION

Opening

- *Open with Prayer.* Pray for courage to embrace repentance as a daily habit that draws us closer to God.

- *Opening Question:* What's a time when God led you to make a meaningful change in your life? What motivated you?

Opening Reflections

- What stood out from Chapters 21–24? Did anything challenge or encourage you?

- How has daily or communal repentance deepened your faith or brought renewal?

Chapter Specific Questions

- *Chapter 21:* Which daily practice (morning prayer, midday check-up, or evening examen) feels most realistic for you to start? How could it shape your spiritual life?

- *Chapter 22:* What impact could corporate repentance have on your church? How might an accountable small group or confession in worship deepen your walk with Christ?

- *Chapter 23:* How does the analogy of checking a rearview mirror help you understand the importance of repentance? What areas of your life might God be asking you to examine?

- *Chapter 24:* Revival begins with repentance. What small steps could you take to foster a spirit of renewal in your own life or church community? How does this inspire your role in sharing the freedom and joy of repentance?

Take Action

- Choose one daily habit of repentance and commit to adding it to your day-to-day life. How could this single step of embracing good guilt help make repentance a regular and life-giving habit? Share with the group how this could transform your life.

Closing Prayer and Encouragement

- Close in prayer: Thank God for the gift of repentance and the freedom it brings. Ask for courage to embrace it and live it out daily.

- Encourage the group: Remind the group that repentance isn't about guilt but transformation. Encourage everyone to take one meaningful step toward renewal this week.

SCAN HERE to learn more about
Invite Ministries—created to invite people to a deeper
faith and living relationship with Jesus Christ